America's Ra

D0150171

The Official Guidebook of the
Durango & Silverton Narrow Gauge Railroad

Table of Contents

The Origin of the
Durango & Silverton Narrow Gauge Railroad

Under the direction of General William Jackson Palmer (1836-1909), the Denver & Rio Grande Railway, founded in 1870, aggressively developed an extensive narrow gauge network throughout Colorado.
Born a Quaker in Pennsylvania, Palmer was awarded the Congressional Medal of Honor for his service in the American Civil War. Palmer was known for his physical stamina, and an ability to overcome adversity. Today historians consider Palmer both a visionary and a pragmatic businessman. Courtesy of the La Plata County Historical Society

The Durango & Silverton Narrow Gauge Railroad runs on a 45-mile extension of track originally called the Silverton Branch. The line was constructed by the Denver & Rio Grande Railway, headed by General William Jackson Palmer, in 1881-82. The mineral riches of Silverton,

deep in the San Juan Mountains, had been their goal since 1876.

A heady optimism existed in America at the time. The Civil War had ended, and settlers and prospectors by the thousands headed to the great Western frontier. Railroads followed the westerly migration, and

1

This dramatic William Henry Jackson photograph taken in the late summer of 1882, just months after the line had been completed to Silverton, shows a Denver & Rio Grande train poised high above the Animas River on the famous High Line.

The large amount of rock debris along the river's edge was caused by the extensive blasting that had been required to create the ledge on which the track sits.

The D&SNGRR

they played a prominent role in shaping our regional and national destiny. Railroad lines brought growth and prosperity wherever they went throughout the West's wide-open spaces.

The transcontinental rail link was completed in Promontory, Utah on May 10, 1869, but the line had bypassed Denver, much to its residents' dismay. The Union Pacific chose the gentler grade to the north, through Cheyenne, Wyoming.

Denver was the gateway to Colorado's mining boom that began with the Pike's Peak gold rush in 1859. Over the next few years, tens of thousands of prospectors swept into the surrounding area, creating the mining communities of Georgetown, Central City, Black Hawk, and Idaho Springs. Fortunes were made for a few individuals, to be sure, but without a rail link from Colorado to the rest of the country, sustained, widespread growth was elusive. Denver's population between 1860 and 1870 grew by only 10 people to 4,759. The Union Pacific, calling itself the Denver Pacific, built a 106-mile spur south to Denver that was completed June 24, 1870. Finally, Denver was a railroad town and other lines began to take notice.

A line built by the Union Pacific's Eastern Division (later known as the Kansas Pacific) connected Denver with Kansas City just a few months after the Denver

Locomotive #1, named the Montezuma, was the first locomotive used by the D&RG, put in service July 3, 1871. The diminutive engine was built in Pennsylvania by the Baldwin Locomotive Works, the same company that built the K-36 class, 480 series, locomotives more than 50 years later. To put its size into perspective, the top of the boiler was just 6 feet off the ground. Locomotives increased in power and size quickly. The locomotive shown above weighed 25,000 pounds; a fully loaded 480 in service today for the D&SNG weighs 286,600 pounds! The Allan C. Lewis Collection

This contemporary photo of the High Line, taken from the same spot as the William Henry Jackson photo on the previous page, shows significant change. The incredible force of high water in the Animas has cleared the riverbed of rock debris, and vegetation has returned to the sides of the canyon. Also notable is the change in size of the locomotives; it took two locomotives to pull six coaches in the earlier photo, while 478, pictured above, regularly pulls ten cars for the D&SNG today.

Recognizing the achievements of the D&RG's civil engineers, led by Thomas Wigglesworth, in constructing the Silverton Branch, the entire line was designated a National Historic Civil Engineering Landmark by the American Society of Civil Engineers in 1968.

Pacific arrived. In charge of that inspired construction effort—151 miles of track were laid in just 92 days—was General William J. Palmer.

Palmer had gained prior experience in railroading while working for the Pennsylvania Railroad before the Civil War. When he arrived in Denver in 1870, Palmer began to envision a railroad heading south from Denver through Santa Fe, New Mexico on to El Paso, Texas, eventually reaching all the way to Mexico City. Palmer quit the Kansas Pacific and began seeking financial backing from private investors in the eastern United States and Europe for his own railroad, the Denver & Rio Grande.

The D&RG began laying track south from Denver on July 28, 1871, and a few months later reached Colorado Springs, a town that Palmer had actually founded. Palmer was always a savvy real estate developer, and he hoped, justifiably, that Colorado Springs would become a center for tourism and recreation. Palmer later retired on the outskirts of the town.

The push continued south to Pueblo, Colorado. Located at the confluence of the Arkansas River and Fountain Creek, Pueblo originated in 1860, and was still a quiet trading post until the railroad arrived. Palmer helped establish steel manufacturing in the town and by the 1880s, Pueblo was a bustling steel center, and even aspired to

replace Denver as the state capitol.

Before steel manufacturing began in Pueblo, the D&RG had been importing steel from Pennsylvania. When the D&RG subsidiary, the Colorado Fuel and Iron Company, became operational in Pueblo, the D&RG was able to cut costs for its 30-pound rail by 50%.

The D&RG, unlike many railroads of its day, did not seek government backing. In those early years Palmer frequently faced financial difficulties that slowed his railroad's construction efforts, but by 1876, crews were ready to cross Raton Pass in southern Colorado. From there they would be able to drop into the Rio Grande River Valley and pursue General Palmer's goal of reaching Santa Fe and beyond.

Plans changed! Throughout Colorado, the D&RG faced increasing competition from other fledgling lines. The Atchison, Topeka & Santa Fe, later known simply as the Santa Fe Railroad, fought hard for domination in Colorado. The Santa Fe had crossed Kansas and reached Pueblo, and by 1876, they too were aiming south for the route over Raton Pass. The Santa Fe crew outraced the D&RG's men to occupy the pass first, ready to use physical force against its rival if necessary. Violence between the two competing railroads did not occur during this episode, but hard feelings between the rivals were destined to erupt within a couple of years. The

This photograph of a D&RG train in 1914 shows the narrow confines of the Royal Gorge. The build-up of the roadbed at the edge of the Arkansas River illustrates the difficulty the railroad had constructing the line through the Gorge. The railroad advertised the dramatic landscape to sightseers. Courtesy of the Salida Regional Library

Santa Fe crews secured the strategic crossing point, thwarting the D&RG's efforts to gain a route over Raton Pass.

Palmer was forced to change directions with his line and head west over rugged terrain, still hoping to reach Santa Fe, but now on a less direct course through the San Luis Valley. In 1877, the D&RG crossed over Dump Mountain at La Veta Pass, between Walsenburg and Alamosa, achieving its first experi- ence with mountain railroading. At the time, no other rail line in North America had been built at such a high elevation—9,242 feet—or with such steep grades, well over 3%. The D&RG was later to tout itself as the railroad that went "Thru the Rockies...Not Around Them."

The spectacular geologic wonder known as the Royal Gorge, west of Pueblo along the Arkansas River, became the focus of both the D&RG and Santa Fe railroads in 1878.

After the huge construction effort through the Royal Gorge, the D&RGW promoted itself as the Scenic Line, with this herald that was introduced in 1926, currently on the front of the Durango Depot. Recently the D&SNG has created a similar slogan: *Scenic Line, Through the San Juans.*

Silver mining in California Gulch, around Leadville, had been developing since 1874, and by 1878, the vast silver deposits there were attracting national attention. For a time, Leadville had the second largest population in Colorado. The D&RG aimed to tap into the huge market there before its rival by building a line on the most direct route west through the narrow, steep Royal Gorge.

In a scene that could have come from Hollywood, Santa Fe informants reportedly overheard D&RG men discussing their plan in a saloon. Santa Fe crews raced to the Gorge in the middle of the night to start setting up survey stakes. When D&RG men discovered the intruders the next morning, fists began flying, portending the showdown that would ensue shortly thereafter.

In the struggle there could be only one winner: the Gorge was the obvious choice for the route west to Leadville, and at only 30 feet wide in spots, it simply did not have the physical space to accommodate more than one line of rails. Crews for both lines hired armed private militias, and staked out heavily defended positions in the Gorge. Whether actual violence occurred is uncertain, but the potential for it certainly existed in the tense standoff.

The battle continued in and out of the courtrooms as well. In 1880, a complex legal ruling between the two railroads was reached that would forever affect the destinies of each line: the Santa Fe agreed not to build west from Cañon City through the Royal Gorge, and the D&RG agreed not to build south, effectively

This pastoral view of the Animas Valley has not changed significantly since construction crews for the D&RG came here in 1881.

ending General Palmer's dream of his railroad reaching Mexico City. The Santa Fe Railroad would later become a major trans-continental line, while the D&RG would forever remain focused on the West, primarily serving Colorado and Utah.

Construction through the Royal Gorge would prove to be challenging and expensive for the D&RG. To recoup some of their expenditures, they later encouraged passenger travel on the famous Scenic Limited that featured a stop in the gorge for sightseers.

The D&RG reached Leadville in July 1880. They would continue to expand service to other mountain mining centers, and the D&RG became known as the "Little Giant of the Colorado Mountains." The D&RG layed narrow gauge lines to land that only ten years earlier had been described as "impenetrable wilderness." The very active con-

struction crews of the D&RG became adept at building at higher elevations, dealing with the harsh weather, as well as the great engineering challenges of the steep environment.

The farthest south the D&RG ever reached was Santa Fe, New Mexico in 1887, and then only as a narrow gauge extension from Chama, New Mexico. The Santa Fe Branch, known affectionately as the Chili Line, had passenger signs written in English and Spanish, but was never prosperous for the D&RG and was abandoned in 1942.

Of the major mining centers in Colorado, only Silverton lacked the vital rail link in 1881. In 1878, the D&RG, led by Thomas Wigglesworth, began surveying in southwest Colorado to determine the best route into the promising, yet forbidding, San Juans. A route through Del Norte, continuing over the Continental Divide near Cunningham Pass north of Silverton was given serious consideration. The more southerly route through Alamosa and up the Animas Valley eventually won out because it could more easily support the coal-burning smelter that was already part of the D&RG's plans.

The D&RG route to Silverton headed in a southerly direction from their base in Denver, through Colorado Springs, Pueblo, and Walsenburg. Then branching westward, rails led to the D&RG hub of Alamosa that had been established in 1878. Years later, Alamosa would be the transition point from the D&RG's standard to narrow gauge lines. In 1880, line crews were beginning to lay rails out of Alamosa on what the railroad called the San Juan Extension, heading south toward Antonito, Colorado — another railroading town that the D&RG founded. In 1881, rails reached Antonito and continued west to Chama, New Mexico, climbing Cumbres Pass at an elevation of 10,022 feet, at the time, the highest point reached by narrow gauge in the United States. Palmer had no way of knowing that during some winters Cumbres Pass received as much as 500 inches of drifting snow that would later prove a huge challenge to D&RG service. From Chama the line continued toward Durango, roughly along the state line between New Mexico and Colorado.

Through early 1881, Durango anxiously awaited arrival of the railroad with town newspapers reporting the progress of the construction crews each week. Tracks were completed to Durango on July 27, 1881. A huge two-day celebration was held on August 5th and 6th when dignitaries, including General Palmer, the Governor of Colorado, and three former Governors, rode the train into town.

D&RG crews had already begun initial work on the final 45-mile stretch to Silverton, and work continued at a rapid pace. The chief engineer for the project was Thomas Wigglesworth, who had plotted the railroad's course from Durango to Silverton in 1879, and would soon play a significant role in developing other southwest Colorado railroads.

The Silverton Branch was the

D&RG's first line built with rails made of steel, rather than iron. The labor force numbered around 500 men, many of them new arrivals to America. They performed the often-dangerous work for an average daily pay of $2.25, considered a decent wage at that time. Rails were laid from Durango through the Animas Valley and up to Rockwood by late fall, and work progressed through the harsh winter of 1881-82.

Construction crews reached Silverton in July 1882, completing the link from Durango to Silverton in an incredible 11 months!

The arrival of the railroad into Silverton, as throughout the American West, had a huge impact. Economic benefits to the area's mining efforts were enormous; freight rates for the all-important mineral ores plunged. Freight taken by wagon over Stony Pass to Del Norte in the 1870s was charged $60 a ton, and that dropped to $30 on toll roads built by Otto Mears. When the railroad arrived, freight rates to the smelter in Durango fell to $12 a ton. Trains boosted mining activity by efficiently supplying the Silverton community with food, household goods, construction materials, and mining supplies. The mining indus-try and the railroad flourished for most of the next 30 years. Silverton's population more than doubled to 2,000 people by 1885.

In 1882, a first-class ticket from Silverton to Denver cost $37.30 — $4 more for a sleeper—and the trip was scheduled at thirty hours. That

Alva Lyons (1897-1990) was a conductor for the D&RGW for over 50 years. He was very knowledgeable, and tirelessly promoted the Silverton Branch, providing passengers with coffee and stories. He was honored with a plaque in the Durango Depot in August, 1991. Southwest Book Trader

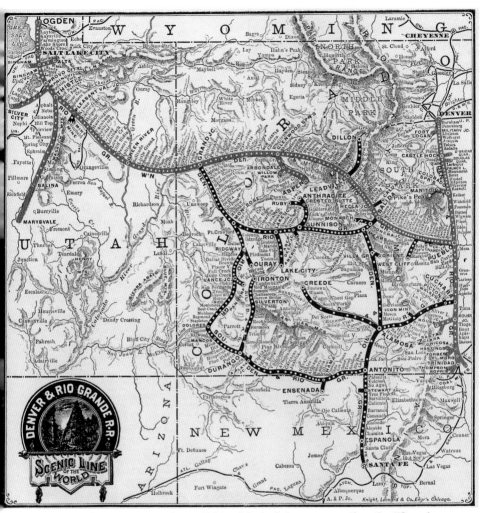

A D&RG system map from 1903, with their logo promoting the "Scenic Line of the World," showed standard gauge lines highlighted in red, while narrow gauge lines were marked black. A standard gauge line from Durango south to Farmington, New Mexico would be builit in 1905.

The route of the Rio Grande Southern, heading northwest from Durango, was considered part of the D&RG system; the RGS had gone into receivership by 1903, and was basically being operated by the D&RG.

seems like a long time to us today, but before the train, the journey by Barlow & Sanderson Stage could take five days!

Of course, not everyone was pleased with the rates charged by the D&RG in Silverton, or anywhere else for that matter. Like modern airlines, the D&RG charged as much as the market would bear. It was often said that a railroad's entry to town was characterized by high hopes followed by high rates.

Although the narrow gauge equipment used by the D&RG was smaller than standard gauge, it did not lack for amenities: parlor cars and dining cars provided the highest levels of comfort and service. Until the years of the Great Depression, sleeper service was provided on the Silverton Branch and passengers could ride from Silverton to Denver, changing trains only in Alamosa, from narrow to standard gauge.

Operation of the Silverton Branch has always been challenging, subject to the whims of Mother Nature. Mudslides, avalanches, blizzards, and floods have periodically interrupted service ever since the railroad's arrival. In the winter of 1883-84, snowdrifts and avalanches blocked the rails for 73 long days. The 45-mile line has been subjected to three so-called "one hundred year" floods of the Animas River. (See more under the heading of the Animas River on page 143).

The fortunes of freight hauling for the D&RG followed the prosperity of the mining industry in general. Ore prices were subject to changes in governmental money policies and other cyclical economic factors. When profits transporting mineral ores diminished in the San Juans after the First World War, the D&RG turned its attentions toward its more lucrative, east-west standard gauge routes. Continuing financial problems and mis-management led to the railroad's re-organization as the Denver & Rio Grande Western in 1921.

During the postwar prosperity of the late 1940s and early 1950s, owning an automobile became an essential part of the American Dream, and the railroad industry was slow to modernize. The rapid spread of highways and automobiles took its toll on railroad business, especially passenger trains, all over the United States. Rail service lasted longer in the San Juans because highways were difficult to build and maintain in this rugged country, and railroads remained the only dependable transportation to the outside world for many small towns throughout the 1940s. But unfortunately for most of the old narrow gauge network, highway expansion did eventually prevail in southwestern Colorado. The long-persevering Rio Grande Southern, another narrow gauge line out of Durango, finally called it quits in 1951, when lucrative mail contracts were lost to truck transportation.

For the same reason, Durango

lost its daily rail connection to Alamosa called the San Juan, better known to Durangoans as the Eastern. The beautifully appointed train had been a fine example of rail travel, featuring steam heat, electric lights, comfortable seating, and parlor cars with tables for five. It was very formal, even though the cook was also the waiter. The San Juan was rarely late; people in Durango used to set their clocks by the 4 p.m. whistle at Wideman's saw mill, the train scheduled into town at 4:05.

Attempts to bolster sagging revenues with tourism began for the D&RGW in the late 1940s. The narrow gauge line west of Alamosa was the last totally steam-powered operation in the country, and familiar to railroading enthusiasts everywhere. Initially tourists were included on "mixed" trains that also included freight cars.

Unlike service between Durango and Alamosa, early passenger service to Silverton was rather primitive. Some of the first coaches used had

Passengers at the Durango Depot are shown boarding the train to Silverton on July 8, 1950. Passenger service, very sparse only a decade earlier, was growing more than the D&RGW wanted. In 1963, the parking lot that was sometimes a jumble of cars, was moved away from the building.
The Allan C. Lewis Collection

seen service on the Chili Line, with toilets identified in Spanish and English. The seats were close together, cars were heated by messy coal stoves instead of steam, and there was no electricity or running water. Toilets were open holes to the ground.

Rail aficionados were willing to put up with a little discomfort and early efforts at tourism proved successful; ridership on the Silverton Branch in 1947, the first year tourists were accommodated, was a respectable 3,444 passengers.

Hollywood discovered the Narrow Gauge Country of southwest Colorado in the early 1950s, and provided more of a boost to tourism than D&RGW marketing could ever afford. In 1950, "A Ticket to Tomahawk", which included Marilyn Monroe, Walter Brennan, Anne Baxter, and Rory Calhoun in its cast, was filmed using the railroad and featuring spectacular locations around Durango and Silverton.

For "A Ticket to Tomahawk", the color of the train was changed to a bright yellow at the request of the movie's producers. The color, that today has its own trademarked-name, Rio Grande Gold, was popular and soon replaced the familiar, but rather drab old standard Pullman Green on the Silverton Branch. All cars had received a fresh coat of paint by 1955. The change added a distinctive and unmistakable identity for the line.

While the setting for another movie, "Across the Wide Missouri", produced in 1951, was Montana, most of the film was actually shot in the San Juan Mountains. That movie cast included the legendary Clark Gable and Ricardo Montalban. The year after saw three more films made in this area: "Denver & Rio Grande", produced by Paramount Pictures, "Viva Zapata", made by 20th Century Fox, and MGM's "Lone Star". More were to follow, notably, "Around the World in Eighty Days", "How the West Was Won", and "Butch Cassidy and The Sundance Kid". All of these films brought attention to the area, and contributed to increased passenger loads on the Silverton Branch.

By the 1950s, mining had slowed (though it still persisted) and the D&RGW sought to abandon much of its remaining narrow gauge system in Colorado, including the Silverton Branch, despite its success with passenger service. In 1962, the railroad filed a petition with the Public Utilities Commission for permission to stop service to Silverton, even though the Silverton Branch generated more revenue than any other passenger train they operated. Like all railroads, the D&RGW operated under the auspices of the Interstate Commerce Commission and the PUC, and could not simply drop a line at will. The PUC heard protests from local residents concerning the profitability of the passenger train here and its historical

During a stop at the Silverton Depot, railfans pose by the Silver Vista in this shot from the early 1950s. In its effort to develop tourism, the D&RGW introduced the glass-topped car to the Silverton Branch in 1947. Unfortunately, it was destroyed in a 1953 fire at the Alamosa car shop, in the same building where it had been built. The D&SNG recently constructed a new Silver Vista, dedicated in May 2006, its design based largely on the original.

significance. Silverton business groups went to Washington, claiming that the mining industry would be ruined without train transportation. The PUC denied the railroad's request and the D&RGW was begrudgingly forced to continue service there.

The train to Silverton had gradually turned into a tourist line instead of a freight-hauler. And, to the great consternation of the D&RGW, tourism continued to grow—passenger numbers in 1963 topped 50,000!

Why the D&RGW wanted to divest itself of all of its narrow gauge lines, even obvious money-makers like the Silverton Branch,

was never totally clear. The railroad even went to great lengths to discourage business on its narrow gauge lines. A Rio Grande bus station was located across the street from the Strater Hotel, and a Rio Grande truck line operated for a while; both were established by the D&RGW to divert business from the railroad. To frustrate local businesses, freight was sometimes allowed to sit on sidings at Arboles and Ignacio just to delay delivery. One possible explanation for the D&RGW's reasoning is that narrow gauge just did not fit into the corporate image they wished to promote during that era. Larger, more mod-

15

ern, trains were in vogue.

Some of their motivation was clear; with a base in Denver and an operation, at this point, riding mostly on standard gauge track, the D&RGW had logistical problems with the Silverton Branch. The last freight train between Alamosa and Durango ran in 1968, and not long after, much of the San Juan Extension was torn up. It became difficult for D&RGW to schedule crews and allocate resources to this "island" of narrow gauge rails between Durango and Silverton. Passenger train overhead is always much higher than freight hauling, and promotion of a tourist, passenger line never became a priority for the D&RGW.

The only other part of the San Juan Extension still in existence runs between Antonito, Colorado and Chama, New Mexico. That portion of the line was purchased jointly by the states of Colorado and New Mexico for historic preservation in 1970. Today it is the location of another tourist line, the Cumbres & Toltec Scenic RR.

Unable to abandon the Silverton Branch, the D&RGW began looking to sell the line during the late 1970s. Finally in 1981, the railroad was successful in its efforts to find a buyer. Charles E. Bradshaw Jr., Florida citrus grower and businessman, purchased the 45-mile line and rolling stock. Bradshaw changed the name of the railroad to the Durango & Silverton Narrow Gauge, and his

Jeffrey D. Jackson, Senior Vice President and Chief Operating Officer for the D&SNG.
Photo by Yvonne Lashmett

commitment to the line was soon evident. Under his ownership, improvements were made to the track and equipment following years of neglect.

Along with the preservation of the railroad's history, Bradshaw wanted a decent rate of return on his investment. More trains were added to the schedule to increase passenger capacity. Passenger numbers on the D&SNG expanded greatly, peaking at around 200,000 annually by the 1990s.

In 1997, Bradshaw sold the D&SNG to First American Railways, Inc. Shortly thereafter, in 1998, the current owners, Carol and Al Harper, purchased the line. The Harpers, founders of American Heritage Railways, have a passion for railroad preservation, and pride themselves on being guardians of

Today the Silverton Branch is probably in the best physical condition of its 125-year history with upgraded rail, rebuilt rolling stock, and overhauled locomotives. To verify that the line is in good shape, the D&SNG brings in an independent structural engineering firm twice a year to inspect the 45-mile line, including all 32 bridges.

the D&SNG. They are now neighbors, having recently moved the headquarters of American Heritage Railways from Florida to Durango. American Heritage Railways also owns the Great Smoky Mountains Railroad based in Dillsboro, North Carolina, that operates in a very scenic part of the Appalachian Mountains near the Great Smoky Mountains National Park.

The D&SNG will always face challenges, as exemplified by the overwhelming fires in 2002. The railroad's management team has proven itself very capable of adjusting to and learning from such unforeseen problems, and the railroad is in good hands. The future looks promising for the D&SNG, as this line has become known worldwide for its unique historical value. Recognizing the importance of maintaining the D&SNG's historic

integrity, the National Park Service designated the entire line a National Historic Landmark in 1967. In 2000, the Society of American Travel Writers honored the D&SNG as one of the Top 10 Most Exciting Train Journeys in the World; but you probably knew that already!

Carol Harper, President, and Allen C. Harper, Chief Executive Officer of the D&SNG.

Photo by Yvonne Lashmett

17

Narrow Gauge

Narrow gauge track in Colorado was laid at a width of 3 feet between rails, instead of the 4 feet-8 1/2 inches of separation with standard gauge rail. *Slim-gauge* was the choice of William Jackson Palmer for several reasons. It was capable of making sharper curves, and thus more suited to the mountainous terrain found in much of Colorado. The rail weighed about 30 pounds a yard, one half that of standard gauge track at the time, so manufacturing costs were lower. The D&RG was also able to operate lighter, less expensive equipment on its narrow gauge lines.

Another important factor favoring narrow gauge rails was its speed of installation. In the early years, the D&RG was competing with other lines to reach the coveted mining camps of Colorado, and time was of the essence. The lightweight 30-pound rail was spiked onto 6-foot long hand-hewn ties that were often laid on bare ground. Under ideal conditions, 15 miles of track could be laid in a single day. D&RG section crews would later return and solidify these lines by adding ballast.

Palmer first became acquainted with narrow gauge rail while on his honeymoon in Great Britain in 1870, when he was drawing up plans for his new railway. He visited the Festiniog Railway that operated at a slate mine in North Wales and ran on tracks just 2 feet wide. The operation there had recently added steam-powered locomotives to supplement their animal-drawn trains.

Palmer saw great promise in narrow gauge for his new line, and under his direction, the D&RG

There is a dramatic difference between the 30-pound rail that was laid originally on the Silverton Branch and today's 85-pound rail.

became the first, and largest narrow gauge railway in North America. By 1888, the D&RG had a network of 1,670 miles of narrow gauge track.

Narrow gauge rail became popular in other parts of the country during the 1870s and 1880s, when railroads found they could reach locations that until then had been too difficult and costly. In Pennsylvania, the East Broad Top Railroad began to serve the rich coalfields of Broad Top Mountain. In Maine, 2-foot gauge tracks were built into logging country, and narrow gauge lines in California and Nevada were developed to carry mining and timber products.

There were logistical problems for the D&RG with narrow gauge rail from the start. It was difficult and costly for the railroad to transfer freight between narrow gauge and standard gauge cars. As manufacturing technology evolved, locomotives became larger and more powerful, but the increased size made it impossible for new locomotives to negotiate the sharp mountain curves where narrow gauge track existed. Nor could the original lightweight

rail support the heavier equipment. These factors, and because so much of the industry remained committed to standard gauge, led the D&RG to begin replacing the original narrow gauge rail in its system as early as the 1880s.

Economics and geography still dictated that some areas of the D&RG system remain narrow gauge, including, of course, the Silverton Branch. The rail here has been upgraded: today all of the rail is at least 65-pound per yard weight and most of it is 85 and 90-pound rail. Some of the original 30-pound rail is still visible along the banks of the Animas River where flooding destroyed the roadbed. Look for the old rails from the High Bridge, Milepost 471.2 to 473 and around MP 474.6.

The light steel rail used in the construction of the Silverton Branch in 1881-82 was the first manufactured by the Colorado Fuel & Iron Company in Pueblo, the only steel mill then in Colorado, and a company that General William Palmer had helped establish.

In this tinted photograph, Jackson's special train is shown heading north along the Animas River with Pigeon Peak in the background.

The D&SNGRR; photo by W.H.Jackson

Master Photographer of the American West

William Henry Jackson is probably the most celebrated photographer of the Western Frontier. Born in Keeseville, New York on April 4, 1843, he served with Union forces in the American Civil War. After that conflict, like so many of his contemporaries, he headed west.

He had practiced portraiture in the Eastern United States and opened a photography studio with two brothers in Omaha, Nebraska in 1868. But Jackson was not happy shooting portraiture and weddings on the prairie. Omaha was on the transcontinental rail link that had been completed in 1859, and Jackson, who had eternal wanderlust, began a train ride toward Salt

Lake City in 1869. He did not have much money at the time and got off the train in towns along the way, taking photos of local residents to pay the way to his next stop. When he finally arrived in Salt Lake City he met Ferdinand V. Hayden, who was conducting a federally funded survey of the West. In 1870, Hayden hired Jackson to help document the expedition and publicize the new American frontier.

On that expedition, Jackson visited locations that were previously unknown to the American people, and his photographs during that period increased public awareness of areas that later became National Parks, including Yellowstone and

The D&RG furnished Jackson with his own well-equipped private car so he could travel with friends and develop his 20x24 inch glass plates. A huge set of elk antlers is mounted on the front of the locomotive. The train is on the High Line near Rockwood. The long, low timber trestle visible in the distance was destroyed by a fire in 1904.

The D&SNGRR; photo by W.H.Jackson

Mesa Verde. During that era, he loaded some 300 pounds of cumbersome photographic equipment, including chemicals and delicate glass plates, onto his trusted burro named Gimlet. When there was no fresh water available for processing his images, he would melt snow.

In August 1873, Jackson photographed Holy Cross Mountain, near today's Vail. The shot dramatically highlighted a snowy cross near the top of the peak and made him famous. The poet Longfellow was sufficiently inspired to write of the finding.

In 1879, Jackson moved to 413 Larimer Street in Denver where he was commissioned by railroads like the Denver & Rio Grande that were hoping to encourage sightseeing and advertise how much easier traveling in the West had become. Between 1880 and 1894, Jackson photographed almost every railroad in the American West. In 1898, he relocated to Detroit where he pioneered efforts in color printing.

William Henry Jackson died in 1942, at 99 years of age. He stayed productive for most of his life and has left us a rich and varied collection of at least 800,000 images documenting the golden era of the American West and his travels around the world.

Durango, Still a Railroad Town!

Durango was a railroad town from its very beginning. The Denver & Rio Grande founded the town in 1880 as a base for operations in southwest Colorado, and their long awaited 45-mile push into Silverton.

The Animas Valley area offered the railroad a relatively hospitable climate and an abundance of the coal they needed to fire their locomotives and to fuel the smelter that was already planned. The town site had good access in all directions to allow future expansion of their rail lines.

Officials of the D&RG borrowed the name Durango from the Mexican town of the same name — Mexicans had earlier taken the name from the Spanish town, Durango! General William Palmer was fluent in Spanish, and his original plans had been to connect the D&RG from Denver all the way south to Mexico City, so the name chosen was probably related to that idea.

When the D&RG arrived in the Animas Valley, it found a small, but thriving settlement already in existence, Animas City. The growing community had been incorporated in 1876 and had its own post office. The town supported the increasing mining activity in the San Juan Mountains to the north with its agricultural products.

The railroad reportedly offered Animas City officials the opportunity to become the new hub of their operations. Some contend that the D&RG's offer was not in earnest because the railroad planned to develop a town on their own property all along. We know that negotiations did not succeed. Rather than build their operations in Animas City, the D&RG simply opted to buy 160 acres of flat, sagebrush covered land along the Animas River to the south, and establish its own town, Durango.

During that era, it was common practice for the D&RG, like many railroad companies throughout America, to build their own new towns. The railroads knew they would attract most businesses in the area anyway, and they would also profit in the sale of land that they owned. This pattern certainly followed here; merchants moved from Animas City to be nearer the downtown depot, and most new development centered on Durango. Animas City never rivaled Durango and was eventually annexed by its larger neighbor in 1948–the train never even stopped there!

The D&RG kept land between the tracks and the Animas River for its own future operations, along with the smelter site and some nearby coalfields. Once it had satisfied its own property needs, the railroad began selling lots in town for $160 each. Surveyors laid out the streets of Durango in the grid system, running north to south and east to west.

In 1895, a bustling Durango was in its early years of development. The ore smelter, in the foreground here next to a substantial pile of tailings, was built in close proximity to the railroad yard, visible just across the Animas River. A spur of track crossed the river downstream, so that side-dump gondolas could be emptied close to the smelter.

As you can see, a huge amount of tailings was generated; much of it was piled up around the smelter, and some was hauled away and used as fill around Durango.

Depending on the direction of the wind, downtown could get quite smokey back then. People put up with it; a century ago, jobs were considered more important than environmental concerns.

A trolley car stands in front of the depot on Main Avenue.

The D&SNGRR

Cowgirls still feel at home in Durango. A rodeo takes place at the County Fairgrounds in the summer. Though their numbers are diminished, cowboys and cowgirls, and the Western culture they represent, still set the style here.

Unlike other railroads in the West, the D&RG never sought, nor received, federal land grants. General Palmer knew his railroad needed the compensation it received by creating nice towns that attracted new residents and businesses, as it had already done in Salida and Colorado Springs. From its original plan, Durango shared some of those towns' amenities—parks, tree-lined sidewalks and traffic islands such as those on East Third Avenue.

Durango grew quickly. By 1881, Durango had become the La Plata County seat, and its population reached 2,500. Railroad Street, with tracks down the middle, was the business center then. With the completion of the line to Silverton a year later, Durango became an important regional site, culturally and economically. Until 1910, Durango was the biggest town on Colorado's western slope.

The vast mineral deposits in Silverton had assured the railroad's success from the start and construction of the smelter in Durango began before the track was even finished. Over the following decades, the capacity of the smelter was increased many times, as was output from Silverton's mines. For many years, Durango's nickname was Smelter City.

Durango and Silverton's fortunes were intertwined. The smelter was the primary employer in Durango, and many local merchants profited supplying the miners to the north. During the first 20 years of the railroad's operation, Durango had a strong local timber industry that met the needs of mining construction.

In the early days, Durango had the classic elements of a Western frontier town: there were shoot-outs between rival gangs, a public hanging, and opium dens. Most men

Cow Girls
on Parade
Durango Fair
& Roundup
9-24-19
(Rowland)
10

The Durango Fair and Roundup, pictured here, was a forerunner of the Navajo Trails Fiesta that was popular with southwest Coloradoans for decades. The name of the celebration has been shortened—today it's called Fiesta Days.

25

Before going on their outing sometime in the late 1890s, the Durango Wheel Club paused for a photograph in this spacious, empty lot across the street from the Strater Hotel. The Durango Wheel Club was formed in 1895, and advocated for improved roads around town. Horses and wagons dominated the byways back then, and roads were mostly rough, and ill-suited for safe, enjoyable bicycling. The Strater Hotel Collection

carried guns around town. There were 20 saloons in Durango five months before the railroad arrived, most with gambling in the back.

The largest of several red-light districts in town existed west of the railroad tracks on two city blocks around 10th Street, complete with saloons, dance halls, and gambling "hells." Houses of prostitution with names like "The Silver Bell" and "The Hanging Gardens of Babylon" thrived here for decades.

Of course, many of Durango's residents were offended by this type of activity and tried to limit its promotion. On October 1, 1889, the Durango City Council issued the following proclamation: "Resolve that the Mayor instruct the City Marshall to stop all fancy women from riding on horseback or in open carriages or otherwise exhibiting or advertising their occupation on the streets of the city of Durango."

Before the turn of the century, laws were passed by the city council outlawing prostitution, but in reality, it was still condoned. Rather than close down the establishments outright, monthly fees were assessed each "working lady." These fees, like taxes, funded many city projects. The last of the "houses of inequity" did not disappear until the 1950s.

Jack Dempsey is still on his feet in this mural painted by Tom McMurry at the corner of Main Avenue and 10th Street. A 10-round bout pitted Dempsey against Andy Malloy, across the street at the Gem Theatre in 1915.

Dempsey was born June 24, 1895 into an impoverished family in the little southwest Colorado town of Manassa. To raise himself out of poverty, starting at age 16, Dempsey fought numerous fights throughout the mining areas of Colorado and Utah, challenging all comers for purses ranging between $2 and $40. He frequently got around on the narrow gauge lines of the D&RG.

Dempsey became heavyweight champ at a lean 187 pounds on July 4, 1919 when he surprised Jess Willard with a withering attack in the first round of their bout.

Durango has become a major destination for bicyclists. It was recently named by *Outside* magazine as the best mountain biking city in the U.S.

As the location of large-scale mining, southwestern Colorado was one of the first areas in the world to have electric power. During the late 1800s, two competing systems, direct current (DC), and alternating current (AC) were vying for supremacy in the public market-place. AC had technical advantages, and eventually became used universally, but only after it had been successfully tested in the San Juans. In 1891, the world's first commercial AC plant was built in Ames, near Telluride, for the Gold King Mine.

Electricity in the form of DC first came to Durango in 1887, produced for a small area of downtown by the Durango Light Company. After the triumph of the power plant in Ames, Durango was among the nation's first municipalities to have AC delivered on a larger scale, in 1893. The Durango Power Plant used locally-mined coal to fuel steam-powered generators, and it supplied energy for local businesses, the hospital, and the previously horse-drawn Main Avenue trolley. The facility was housed in a unique, Mission-style building, the oldest plant of this type in the world, and is now being converted into the Durango Discovery Museum.

In 1906, nearby Mesa Verde became the tenth National Park in

Trolley service began in Durango as a horse-pulled operation in 1891, and became electrified by late 1892. The service was never very prof-itable—the charge was a nickle per ride. The trolley lasted 30 years, and eventually connected the downtown depot with Animas City near 32nd Street. Today a trolley-styled, diesel-powered bus has taken over that route.
The Strater Hotel Collection

The architecture of the Strater Hotel, completed in 1888, is termed *Victorian Eclectic*, incorporating a combination of detail elements that were popular in Colorado from 1870 to 1900. The semi-circular arch over this window is *Romanesque*, while the highly decorative gingerbread detail is known as the *Queen Anne* style of architecture.

Durango has preserved much of its architectural history. After a major fire destroyed many blocks of wooden buildings in 1881, including the city hall and courthouse, the City of Durango required that rebuilding in the burned area be done with brick or stone. Many of the buildings constructed since then remain.

The Main Avenue commercial area and East 3rd Avenue are designated National Historic Districts, and neighborhoods around the old downtown retain much of their original charm and authenticity.

Durango has always had neighborhoods that are shared by elegant, large homes and the more modest dwellings of working people. These old neighborhoods show a rich variety of architectural styles.

the United States, due largely to the efforts of a Colorado women's group. National interest in the area began with William Henry Jackson's photographs of the ancient cliff dwellings in 1893. The publicity was the initial catalyst for tourism in southwestern Colorado.

Another important archaeological site was found even closer to Durango in the Falls Creek area that lies just above the Animas Valley. It was the home of Ancestral Puebloans nearly 2,500 years ago. Nineteen mummified human remains in extremely good condition were found in a cave there, considered to be the oldest site ever discovered in the Southwest.

After the mid-1910s, mining began to subside in the San Juans due to a decline in demand for gold and silver, and because many mines around Silverton had played out. In 1930, the Durango smelter closed and over 200 local citizens lost their jobs. Throughout the Great Depression of the 1930s, the Durango economy suffered, but it also became more diversified, relying increasingly on agriculture, ranching, and timber harvesting in addition to smaller scale mining.

Rail construction out of Durango did not stop with the line to Silverton. Otto Mears, who played a prominent part developing all of Colorado, formed the Rio Grande Southern—another narrow gauge line—in 1891. The RGS, that later became a subsidiary of the Rio Grande, gave Durango a link west to the mining towns of Telluride, Ophir, and Rico. In 1905, the D&RG added a rail line south to Farmington, New Mexico, originally built as standard gauge and later changed to narrow gauge. (See page 170).

Until the early 1950s, Durango was connected to almost 600 miles of narrow gauge track run by the D&RGW and the RGS. Durango was truly the heart of America's Narrow Gauge Railroading.

For most residents here, like all across America, life revolved around the railroad. Things began to change after World War II, as middle class Americans increasingly flocked to the automobile. Meanwhile, the D&RGW began its efforts to abandon narrow gauge lines and highways replaced rails in every direction, except, of course, the line north to Silverton.

Durango witnessed another mineral boom in the 1940s and 1950s, this time, for uranium and natural gas. The local workforce grew as the Durango smelter was reopened to process uranium ore. Companies that worked the San Juan Basin in New Mexico for natural gas—a huge enterprise still today—had their headquarters in Durango.

Today, Durango remains an important cultural source in southwestern Colorado, greatly enhanced by the presence of Fort Lewis College. Originally an army post located near Hesperus, west of

Coinciding with the 125th year of railroading on the Silverton Branch, in 2006, was the 100th anniversary of Mesa Verde National Park. The two are closely linked as the most popular tourist destinations in southwestern Colorado. The photographs of William Henry Jackson garnered publicity for both. The 4-story structure pictured here is called Square Tower House.

Durango, Fort Lewis became an Indian School to educate and "civilize" Indians, beginning in 1891, and later an Indian Boarding School under the direction of the U.S. Department of the Interior. In 1927, the Colorado General Assembly designated Fort Lewis a two-year college. Fort Lewis was relocated to the mesa overlooking Durango in 1956, when it was changed from a two to a four-year college. Current enrollment is over 4,000.

Durango's history mirrors much

The old and the new converge in downtown Durango.

of the American West's. Extractive industries, such as mining, which brought the railroad here in the first place and provided the basis for the area's initial development, have, to a great extent, disappeared. Today's economy relies heavily on tourism and real estate. The mountains that provided our ancestors with mineral wealth are valued today for their scenic beauty and recreational opportunities.

After a visit to the area in 1935, beloved American humorist Will Rogers said of Durango, "It's out of the way, and darn glad of it." Today Durango is not as out of the way as it once was, and over the last decade residents have witnessed dramatic change.

Like just about every nice place in the country, Durango has experienced a real estate boom. The town's population has climbed to about 14,000, with over 40,000 inhabitants in La Plata County.

Many newcomers are retirees who enjoy the quality of life that Durango offers.

One of the challenges facing the town is how to preserve the cultural and ethnic diversity that has always existed here with home prices escalating out of the reach of folks who actually work here. But most residents and local businesses, like the D&SNG, really care about this community and want to see its multi-ethnic, small-town character preserved.

In keeping with its heritage, there is little glitzy or pretentious here. Durango is still a real town! As one of the last places in the world where one can routinely hear the sounds of a working, steam-powered train, Durango is unique and special to many people. The town has changed in many ways, but it remains a great railroading town, and for that, Durango has earned worldwide distinction.

Cinco de Mayo is celebrated in an area that was once the neighborhood *Santa Rita*, formerly home to many of Durango's Hispanic families. Adjacent to the smokey smelter where many of the residents worked, and next to the Animas River that was then quite polluted, the environment in Santa Rita was challenging, but it was a real community; many of the homes there had gardens.

Absent in the foreground of this recent photograph of Durango is the smelter, illustrating the demise of the regional mining industry. Before it was abandoned, the smelter processed, in 1943, the vanadium ore that was used in the world's first atomic bomb, manufactured in nearby Los Alamos, New Mexico. The radioactive tailings remained here, near the Animas River, until they were moved to safer storage by the Environmental Protection Agency in a huge excavation project during the 1980s.

From a distance, the Missionary Ridge fire looked beautiful and benign in its early stages. The summer of 2002 turned into one of the most difficult, challenging periods in the 125-year history of the Silverton Branch.

The Great Fires of 2002

The largest fire in southwest Colorado's recorded history started on June 9, 2002, after a prolonged, record-breaking drought. Weather statistics for the six months prior to the blaze show the driest span in Colorado for more than a century. The fire started when the hot tailpipe of a vehicle ignited some parched grass along the road to Missionary Ridge, adjacent to the Animas Valley, north of Durango. The fire was reported promptly, and a helicopter was dispatched to extinguish the blaze, but thick smoke prevented the chopper from getting very close and the fire grew rapidly in the extreme, dry conditions.

More than 1,200 firefighters from all over the country battled the Missionary Ridge blaze. The fire consumed over 70,000 acres–almost three times larger than the previous record-holder, the Lime Creek Burn of 1886. Before the fire was contained, 56 homes and 27 outbuildings were destroyed, and 2,300 homes were evacuated.

For the first time in its long history, the D&SNG voluntarily shut down operations to Silverton during the height of its season due to extreme fire danger. The decision made by American Heritage Railroad CEO Al Harper was not an easy one, as many jobs and businesses are threatened when the railroad doesn't run. Local business losses that year were reported to be 30%. Losses for the D&SNG, which does 80% of its business during the short summer season, were devastating. The railroad estimated it lost over $4 million that year from missed passenger revenue alone. Add to that $500,000 for new equipment that was purchased to deal with the fire, and $700,000 reim-

This was a view of the Missionary Ridge fire in all its awesome power from Falls Creek, an area that also ignited in a furious fire just days later.

bursed to the U.S. Forest Service for fire suppression.

Throughout the previous winter, Maintenance of Way (MOW) crews worked on high-risk areas clearing brush and creating firebreaks. These areas include the steeper terrain heading to Rockwood and north of stops at Tank Creek, and Needleton, where the engines work hard, throwing off more cinders. But these measures were no match for the drought conditions that summer. Fire patrols extinguished scores of small fires started by coal-burning locomotives along the railroad's right-of-way.

The railroad added special sprayers to engine smoke stacks to mist the exhaust and cinders passing through the spark arrestors. A box-car that sits behind the locomotive and coal tender car, ahead of the passenger coaches, was loaded with firefighting equipment, and 1,000 gallons of water to quickly suppress any fires. The D&SNG purchased their first diesel engine in 2002 to be used as a stopgap measure to replace the steam locomotives and keep the train running when fire danger is too high.

The railroad had disaster insurance but had to file a lawsuit against insurance companies that tried to withhold compensation. The railroad eventually won the case and the insurance companies had to settle, providing the D&SNG with a much-needed boost in operating revenue.

The railroad anticipated the potential danger of the dry conditions long before the fires struck in 2002, but the severity of the drought was unprecedented. The 2002 fires taught management at the D&SNG some hard lessons, but today they are better prepared than ever before to anticipate and deal with fire.

Bells and Whistles

The distinctive, beautiful bells on D&SNG locomotives were cast from a mixture of brass, bronze, copper, and tin—a combination that offers durability and quality of sound. The fireman rings the bell as a general warning just before the whistle signals the locomotive's movement in the yard, at street crossings, train stations, and while passing other trains.

Five-chime whistles made of brass, and originally manufactured for the D&RG, are on most of the locomotives now operating for the D&SNG. Because the D&SNG did some serious collecting, the whistles' evocative sounds are similar on all D&SNG locomotives.

The whistle is used to signal the locomotive's movements to the rest of the train crew and anyone else in hearing range.

In the following description of the most common signals, long whistles are designated "—", and short whistles "•".

— : One long whistle means that the train is approaching a station, or flag stop, like Rockwood, asking if passengers need to get on or off. After the conductor or brakeman has replied with hand signals, the engineer will then respond with one of the following:

• • : Indicates an affirmative response to a hand signal, and proceed.

• • • : If stopped, backing up; if moving, getting ready to stop.

— — • — : This is the commonly heard warning used at public road crossings.

— • : Another warning whistle, this signal is used when the engineer's view is obstructed and at private crossings.

• : Apply brakes for a brake test; stop. This is done with blue flags on the front of the locomotive to warn others that a brake test is occurring.

— — : Release brakes; start or proceed. This is usually a rather quiet signal done during a brake test.

When the train stops, the brakeman will disembark to the rear of the train to warn approaching traffic. Sometimes the train needs to be protected from both directions, so there are different signals calling for a trainman's return:

— — — — : Return from the west (Silverton side) of the train.
Or:
— — — — — : Return from the east (Durango side) of the train.

The most important signal for you to remember is:

— — — — : Your train in Silverton is getting ready to leave and you must be back in your seat in ten minutes!

Railroad watches, like this beautiful Hamilton, were made to specific standards set by the railroading industry after the 1890s to ensure precision after inaccurate timing resulted in disasters.
D&SNG train crews synchronize their watches to within 30 seconds every morning.

The Journey: Highlights and Insights

The Durango Depot is located at Mile Post 451.52 and the Silverton Depot, near the end of the line, at MP 496.7. The numbers indicate the distance from the Denver & Rio Grande's base in Denver along the original line of track, most of which no longer exists.

Your Durango based train is considered westbound, and the return eastbound, even though, as the map shows, Silverton lies basically north of Durango. In the early years of the D&RG, any train leaving their base in Denver was usually headed west, so westbound became accepted ter-

The mile posts are located on the east side of the tracks, but are visible from trains heading in either direction.

minology within the D&RG for any train heading away from their base, and the tradition continues here for the D&SNG.

From a vantage point overlooking the railroad yard in Durango, the dispatcher (chief dispatcher Dave Schranck shown here), has authority over all movement on the tracks, staying in radio contact with trains, patrol cars, and maintenance of way crews to ensure proper separation between vehicles.

The safe operation of your train is the primary concern of all crew members, and the D&SNG is justifiably proud of its outstanding safety record.

The map on the opposite page is meant to give a sense of the distances between just a few of the notable spots along the 45-mile route between Durango and Silverton.

451

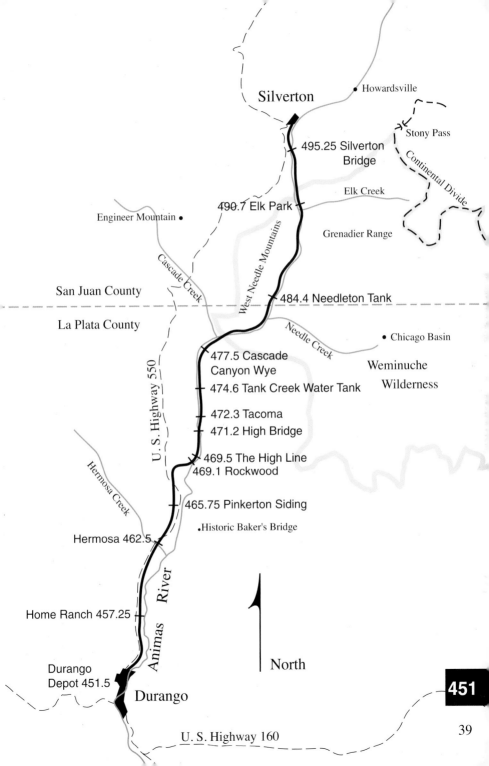

Silverton

• Howardsville

495.25 Silverton
Bridge

Stony Pass

Continental Divide

Elk Creek

490.7 Elk Park

Engineer Mountain •

Grenadier Range

Cascade Creek

West Needle Mountains

San Juan County

484.4 Needleton Tank

La Plata County

Needle Creek

• Chicago Basin

477.5 Cascade
Canyon Wye

Weminuche
Wilderness

474.6 Tank Creek Water Tank

U. S. Highway 550

472.3 Tacoma

471.2 High Bridge

469.5 The High Line
469.1 Rockwood

465.75 Pinkerton Siding

Hermosa Creek

•Historic Baker's Bridge

Hermosa 462.5

River

North

Home Ranch 457.25

Animas

Durango
Depot 451.5

Durango

451

U. S. Highway 160

39

451.52: Our journey begins in the Durango Yard at an elevation 6,520 feet above sea level.

Before your locomotive is coupled to the waiting passenger cars, the fireman and engineer normally arrive about an hour before departure time to do a general inspection. The locomotive is usually waiting for them in front of the coal dock with the tender already full of water and coal. The engine crew "oils around" and cleans off the locomotive. The two water glasses in the cab that show the water level in the boiler are checked to determine that they are working properly. The fireman makes sure the level in the

sand dome, located on top of the locomotive, is adequate for the day's journey; sand is released from the forward dome of the locomotive directly in front of the driving wheels, assisting traction on wet, slippery rails.

When inspections of the locomotive are complete, the crew will climb aboard and proceed to the back of the yard to "blow out" the messy condensate, soot and cinders that have collected overnight in the smoke box and flues. This helps to limit the amount of cinders that are dislodged around the passenger boarding area.

The conductor and his train crew of one or two brakemen normally arrive at least an hour before the train's departure to review the track warrant issued by the dispatcher, describing activity on the right of way to Silverton, and to help with passenger boarding. At the ticket office, they are advised of any passengers with special needs.

The area around the Durango Depot has seen significant change. The Telluride Iron Works was situated where the movie theatre is today. The foundry there made gear pulleys and many items for the railroad. The Durango Hotel once occupied the space where the parking lot is today, across the street from the Depot.

451

451.52: The Durango Depot is the original structure that was built by the railroad while the line to Silverton was being constructed. The depot was completed in January, 1882, and its impressive appearance has changed little since then. The building's large size indicates the volume of business that the D&RG anticipated from the start.

Locomotive 315 (now on display at Durango's Santa Rita Park, and undergoing a nearly completed renovation) is shown moving cars in the late 1940s. The Durango Yard at one time extended west to the Animas River and south back to the area now covered by Highway 160/550. Until the 1950s, tracks headed south, east, and west in addition to the line heading north to Silverton. The Yard had its own coal tipple and water tank until the 1960s when they were dismantled to make way for high way expansion. Prominent Perins Peak overlooks Durango from the west. It was named for Charles Perin, the surveyor of the original Durango town site. The Allan Lewis Collection; photo by R. W. Richardson

451

Railroads have always been artistically inspiring: nationally recognized watercolor artist Russell Steele specializes in paintings of the D&SNG. Russell has become a welcome and familiar sight outside of the Durango Depot.

For many years the Graden flour-mill sat where the Doubletree Hotel is today. Swimming holes behind the mill were often frequented by locals. T. C. Graden, whose relatives owned the mill, was an early settler in the Animas Valley and a friend of General Palmer. At Palmer's request, Graden set up a sawmill to cut ties for the new line to Silverton.

The first mile out of the station takes you through the heart of Durango's old downtown. You pass behind the landmark Strater Hotel in the first block.

There is a link to the past at 8th Street; look for an old painted advertisement on the stately Newman building's west wall, fac-ing the train, posted by the long-gone Smelter National Bank.

Looking east at 9th Street, you see the old buildings of the First National Bank, and across Main, the old Burns National Bank. Both structures were built of quarried stone and are fine examples of late 1880s architecture.

As tracks cross 12th street, to the west you can see the old power plant, the Durango Gas & Electric Company substation, now converted to a Discovery Museum. One hundred years ago you might have seen the teepees of visiting Utes across the river here and also to the east in Buckley Park, off Main Avenue.

452

The old siding and spur called the North Yard or the Uptown Yard, between 8th Street and 12th Street, had been active long ago, but was used to store seldom used and damaged freight cars since the 1960s. The area became a fire hazard, and the D&SNG sold the property and the old cars that sat there in 2004. The area is now used for parking cars.

452.4: The 15th Street Bridge is a through-truss bridge, 246 feet long, with a wooden deck over steel girders. Floods have caused destruction here several times (see page 122); the original bridge at this location was built in 1881 and was damaged by a spring flood in 1885. Another more powerful flood in 1911 washed away a large wooden section of the trestle. The railroad replaced it with this metal-framed bridge.

Just to the west as you cross the 15th Street Bridge is the Colorado State Fish Hatchery. Originally a private hatchery built in 1890, the Colorado Division of Wildlife purchased the facility around 1900.

Today it is capable of raising over a million trout a year to stock the waters of southwest Colorado.

452.85: After passing behind Durango's old Mercy Hospital, tracks cross a wooden bridge over Junction Creek. Like many smaller waterways in southwest Colorado, Junction Creek, whose headwaters are in the La Plata Mountains, normally runs rather placidly except during spring runoff when it can become quite a torrent.

North of Junction Creek are the athletic fields of the Durango High School. The revamped La Plata County Fairgrounds and the Durango Recreation Center lie just

452

north of the High School.

453.9: At the crossing signal, the rails intersect 32nd Street. This was the heart of old Animas City, a settlement that existed before Durango was established by the D&RG in 1880. Main Avenue through Animas City was once a beautiful road lined with white picket fences. Several blocks away, at 3065 West 2nd Avenue, is the Animas Museum, previously a schoolhouse, and the largest building ever built in Animas City. A visit to the museum complements your stay in southwest Colorado.

454.3: 36th Street crossing.

455 – 463: This eight-mile section of the line takes you from Durango's city limits through the beautiful Animas Valley. While the valley is seeing more and more human impact, much of the natural environment remains.

The broad valley was created by glacial activity that took place about 10,000 years ago–not long in geologic time. As you enter the valley, the low-lying hills to the southeast are evidence of a terminal moraine—deposits that mark the end of a glacier's path. To the west is Animas Mountain, and if you look closely, you will see evidence of geologic change in the stratifications of rock.

455.9: United Campground.

456.0: The Iron Horse Inn.

457.25: Home Ranch siding.

458.3: The Falls Creek Bridge. On the west side of the valley is a waterfall, most noticeable in the

457.25: Home Ranch Siding, shown here during Railfest activity, lies adjacent to the glider field in the Animas Valley. The siding was built in 1982 to accommodate increased train traffic of the D&SNG. A hundred years earlier, Home Ranch was a designated stop on the D&RG's first timetable out of Durango, when 70 acres were under cultivation here.

The Trimble Hot Springs Collection

460.7: The train crosses Trimble Lane. Across the highway to the west is Trimble Hot Springs. A hotel opened here in 1882, and Trimble Springs was a popular destination for passengers on the railroad. It was advertised to be a "positive cure for... all diseases that flesh is heir to."

The healing waters of Trimble Hot Springs had long been known to the Utes and their predecessors. The area was used for ceremonial and spiritual gatherings until the mid-1800s. Later, weary miners frequented the springs. Aspirin was not available until 1899, so before that, miners had two options available to ease their aches and pains—hot springs or whiskey!

The impressive Hermosa House, a three-story brick building, is shown in the slightly embellished painting above. It was burned to the ground on July 30, 1931. Fate has not been kind to hotels here: there were two other disastrous fires, in 1892, and in 1957. Today Trimble Hot Springs is once more open for business—and yet another hotel is planned for construction nearby.

458

spring, that is fed by Falls Creek. The area above the waterfall was a refuge for Ancestral Puebloans centuries before the first Spanish explorers or French trappers came through the Animas Valley. The cliffs above Falls Creek were the site of an important archaeological find in the late 1800s.

460.25: Hanks Curve, named for the Hanks family that has owned property here since the 1880s. They have done a little gold mining here. The Hanks' home is built upon a concrete block garage to protect them from flooding in the valley.

460.7: Trimble Lane, an old road that connects the east and west sides of the valley.

462.52: After you cross a small wooden trestle over Hermosa Creek, you are at the site of the old town of Hermosa, a Spanish word meaning pretty, which is certainly justified in describing this setting.

The first settlers arrived here in 1873, and a post office was established in 1876, five years before the arrival of the railroad. At that time, mail from the rest of the world was routed through Del Norte, Colorado, then over Stony Pass to Silverton, and finally into Hermosa along the Animas Canyon Toll Road that was built in 1876-77. Back then mail was delivered once or twice a month if the weather was good.

Railroad construction workers set up a camp here in 1881, when the line progressed out of Durango.

(Continued on page 49)

Winter pasture that is essential to elk is disappearing rapidly in the Animas Valley. As soon as the snowpack melts in the upper San Juans, the elk will return to the high country.

460

The Environment

Durango, at 6,500 feet elevation, lies in the transitional area between the piñon-juniper and the montane ecological zones. These zones do not have distinct boundaries. In southwest Colorado local conditions can vary dramatically depending on elevation and the amount of moisture received. The drier piñon-juniper ecosystem that generally ranges from 5,500 to 7,000 feet, south and west of Durango typically receives 15-20 inches of annual precipitation. Summers are hot and dry and most vegetation is drought tolerant, though recent dry spells have been too severe for many old trees.

Many species of wildlife, like the wild turkey pictured here, find shelter in the dense foliage of shrubs like scrub oak (or Gambel oak), mountain mahogany and serviceberry. This vegetation also produces an abundance of edible seeds, nuts, and berries.

The wild turkey is one species of wildlife that is thriving today in southwest Colorado. It was favored for designation as our national bird by Ben Franklin.

Photo by Michael Serrafin

Among the long list of animals that you may see along the route to Silverton, depending on the time of year, are: elk, mule deer, black bear, Rocky Mountain sheep, coyotes, mountain lion, foxes, beaver, jack rabbits, marmots, jays, bluebirds, and magpies. Lynx, long-legged members of the cat family, have been re-introduced to southwest Colorado and are known to traverse the Silverton Branch, though they are elusive. There is a healthy herd of mountain goats around Chicago Basin.

Many animal species in the Colorado Rockies have no permanent habitat. In summer they move to higher elevations where food and cover is plentiful and they return to warmer, lower elevations in winter.

Curious mule deer, named for their large ears, can often be seen from the train. They are common around the edges of forests where shrubs and brush are plentiful.

462

The Environment

The Animas River shows ancient meandering patterns and oxbows. Evidence of the 2002 fires is visible above the red sandstone cliffs.

Water is a precious resource in the Southern Rockies, as has been made painfully obvious during the recent drought and fires. The Animas River has created a distinct riparian zone all along its corridor, a kind of oasis in this semi-arid environment. These watery zones, including the edges of mountain streams like Tank Creek, Elk Creek, and Junction Creek, while not comprising much in total area, support more plant and animal species than any other ecosystem in the Southern Rockies.

The Animas River has influenced a wide area in the glacially formed Animas Valley. Native cottonwoods and willows flourish on the valley floor along the riverbanks, but the area is being invaded by non-native vegetation like the Russian olive tree that can quickly disrupt habitat for many native species of plants and wildlife.

Bird species thrive in the Animas Valley; Bald eagles can be spotted perching in the cottonwoods along the river's banks in the winter, and red-tailed hawks frequently soar above the valley. Canada geese are common near the Home Ranch siding. The wetlands that surround the riverbed provide habitat for mallards, mergansers, and golden-eye ducks. Numerous migratory birds also visit the valley.

The rather lush riparian zones also appeal to humans. Residential development in the Animas valley is conflicting with the winter habitat needs of migratory elk herds.

462

For many years the Animas Valley threatened derailments because the track was poorly supported on the often soggy valley floor. That whole portion of the line was replaced with heavier rail and increased ballast by D&SNG crews during the 1980s.

Ballast, in railroad terminology, refers to gravel or crushed rock that is placed around and under wooden ties to prevent their shifting when rails are stressed by the load of heavy locomotives. The gravel also allows water to drain away from the ties.

When the D&RG arrived, about 150 people lived in Hermosa.

Although there are no known photographs, we know of conditions at the Hermosa camp from a report by Ernest Ingersoll (who later collaborated with photographer William Henry Jackson) for

Harper's magazine. Ingersoll described framed houses that were provided for some of the supervisors, while laborers stayed in primitive huts only three logs high, resting on bare ground!

Years before the arrival of the railroad, Hermosa served as a center

462

462.5: The old wooden water tank in Hermosa, one of only two remaining on the Durango-Silverton line, has been structurally stabilized but is not operational at this time. Water is currently drained out of a converted tank car when needed. The D&RG built this wooden water tank at Hermosa so engine crews could fill their tenders one last time before heading up the long hill from here to Rockwood.

for farmers who were sending their produce to the thousands of miners around Silverton. The railroad's arrival in November 1881 increased the market for produce, dairy, and livestock in Silverton. Vegetables of all sorts and apples from Hermosa orchards were shipped via the D&RG. One location near Hermosa was known, optimistically, as the "Frost-Proof Ranch."

The D&RG at one time had a small depot, bunkhouse, and section foreman's house near the Hermosa siding.

Hermosa is still important to the railroad; the Hermosa Yard is head-quarters for the D&SNG's mainte-nance of way crew and holds a large

inventory of equipment and supplies.

462.7: The signal at the crossing of U.S. 550 incorporates state-of-the-art, motion-detecting technology.
A symbol of the D&SNG's com-mitment to safety, highway gates were added to the signal in 2001, after 30 accident-free years at the intersection.

462

The Animas Valley provides excellent pasture for horses. Many of the horses work in the high country during hunting season. For many years, there were more horses than people in La Plata County.

A "Spray Train" consisting of Diesel #2, a tank car filled with 7,000 gallons of water, and caboose #0540, was first used during the summer of 2002 to wet down the area adjacent to the tracks before the first train pulled up the steep Hermosa Hill. Hermosa Hill is the most fire-prone area on the line, as the locomotives are pulling hard and releasing lots of cinders.

The D&SNG uses the Spray Train during the dry fire season, and any time conditions warrant. Two unusual tank cars that had been used to transport oil from the San Juan Basin near Farmington to a refinery in Salt Lake City were converted to water cars by the D&SNG in 2002.

462

462.8: The grade changes abruptly after crossing Highway 550, from 1% to a steady, challenging 2 1/2%. The 6 1/2-mile climb up Hermosa Hill, and on to Rockwood, is not only steep, but it is curvy, which increases friction between rails and wheels, and compounds the drag of the coaches behind the locomotive.

As the train gains elevation, look for beautiful views of the Animas Valley.

There is an immediate change in vegetation; the cottonwoods of the Animas Valley give way to the Piñon pine, juniper, Gambel oak, and Ponderosa pine typical of drier country.

463.3: Locke's mountain crossing.

464.6: Patrol car set-off.

465.75: Pinkerton Siding was built in 1982 by the D&SNG, under the direction of Charles Bradshaw, to provide another passing place for trains. It lies on land that James Harvey Pinkerton and his family homesteaded south of Baker's Bridge, on both sides of the river in 1875.

The Pinkerton family worked hard producing dairy products for the mining camps that were springing up in the San Juans. It was reported that in the spring of 1876 they sold 116 pounds of butter for a dollar a pound to miners around Silverton. James Pinkerton became a La Plata County judge in the 1870s before moving to Georgia.

462

During this climb your locomotive will remain at full power, with a noticeable change in its sound. The fireman has been anticipating this change in grade for the last two miles, getting the boiler full of water and the fire burning "white hot!"

The southernmost gate to the old Animas Canyon Toll Road (also called the Wrightman Brothers' Toll Road) passed through the Pinkerton's property. A small settlement there, started by the Baker party around 1860, was called Animas City. The early settlement contained around 50 cabins but only lasted for a few years. It existed long before the second Animas City was established in 1876, close to present day Durango. Pinkerton was able to utilize some of the old log structures left there. One was moved and became a schoolhouse.

Several hot springs are located on the old Pinkerton Ranch, some visible from the highway below. The water's temperature is not as high as the springs on Trimble Lane, but "Pinkerton in the Pines" provided swimming and entertainment for years. Soda water from the springs was bottled and sold as a cure for all diseases in the 1890s.

In August 1880, Chief Ouray of the Utes, who had negotiated seven years earlier with Otto Mears for the mining country in the San Juans, stopped at the Pinkerton Ranch on his way to the tribal reservation in Ignacio, Colorado, about 30 miles

465

southeast. He was ill at the time and died in Ignacio later that same month at the age of 47. The location of his burial site, on a rock mesa south of Ignacio, was kept secret for the next 45 years.

As the train passes Pinkerton siding, you are positioned above historic Baker's Bridge. Charles Baker led the first band of prospectors into the San Juans in 1860, and they wintered in this portion of the Animas Valley. A log bridge was built over the Animas River that continued to be used for half a century. The highway bridge was built just south of the original bridge site.

Baker's Bridge was near the site of a spectacular jump in the movie "Butch Cassidy and the Sundance Kid," starring Paul Newman and Robert Redford. In the movie, the two appeared to leap from a cliff into the river far below, but that scene was aided by skillful Hollywood editing. Today, local youths take the same dangerous jump into the river on hot summer days.

Robert Leroy Parker, alias "Butch Cassidy," robbed his first bank in nearby Telluride, Colorado in 1889. In partnership with Harry Longbaugh, known as the Sundance Kid, the colorful duo staged many successful train and bank robberies throughout the West, including several in Colorado.

467: The train crosses under the U.S. Highway 550 overpass that was built in the late 1970s. This is a favored spot for photographers seeking to get a shot of the train chugging up to Rockwood.

467.3: Patrol car set-off.

467.5: This area is called the "Mini-High Line."

468.1: The tracks cross County Road 250 that used to be a part of US Hwy 550. Below, to the east, is the privately-owned Shalona Lake. The picturesque lake is fed by Elbert Creek, named for Samuel H. Elbert, a pioneer in the area who served as Governor of the Colorado Territory in 1873-74.

Just up the hill west of the tracks is the old Rockwood Quarry that was in use before the turn of the 19th century and had its own spur of track.

468.2: Granite Point.

468.65: Elbert Creek Bridge.

469.1: This is the important flag stop of Rockwood. Like Hermosa, Rockwood was an established community with its own post office years before the railroad's arrival.

Early settlers used the area for livestock grazing and timber-harvesting; local hillsides provided

465

468.2: This photograph shows the train reflecting on Shalona Lake with locomotive 481 heading into the sharp curve at Granite Point. That curve was the site of an eastbound train wreck on January 21, 1917.

The accident, in which there were no serious injuries, was referred to by local newspapers as the *Millionaire's Special* because on board that day were prominent businessmen interested in purchasing the legendary Sunnyside Mine in Silverton. The entire train slid down the snowy hillside. Two passenger cars were destroyed by a fire that started when a coal-burning stove in one of the coaches was knocked over.

The locomotive on that train, T-12 class 169, is currently being restored in Alamosa, Colorado, along with Business Car B-1 that was also involved in the train wreck that day.

Another D&RG coach, then known as Business Car N, was seriously damaged in this wreck. The car was repaired and soon returned to service. Years later it was converted into the D&SNG's private car *Nomad*. More about the Nomad on page 166.

469

Aspen groves share a single root system and are considered the largest and oldest living organisms on earth. A grove can survive for more than 10,000 years!

Aspen stands are usually moist and resist burning. Because they reproduce along a system of shallow lateral roots, they are quick to spread and reestablish after a fire, whereas conifers have to reseed. Conifers displaced many aspen groves during the past century, when the widespread policy in forest management was to suppress wildfires. Today many natural fires are allowed to burn freely where they don't threaten humans, and aspens will likely increase in proportion to conifers.

Because aspen groves are so different than conifer stands, they serve an important ecological role. They provide wonderful habitat for grasses and shrubs, along with an abundance of wildflowers, including arnica, paintbrush, and lupines. Many animals favor aspen stands; deer and elk eat their soft, young sprouts.

many of the rough-hewn ties for the line to Silverton. The settlement in Rockwood, named for pioneer Thomas Rockwood, disturbed the Utes, who had long enjoyed the area's abundant hunting and fishing. A violent outbreak would surely have occurred here had it not been for the intervention of the diplomatic Ute Chief Ouray.

Rockwood was a primary supply point for a 35-mile toll road to the silver-mining town of Rico. The wagon road was busy until the Rio Grande Southern line reached Rico

469

This photo of Rockwood was taken in 1925. When the D&RG opened the Silverton Branch in 1882, the community of Rockwood had its own saloons, depot, hotel, and school. The old school house remains today, several hundred yards north of the tracks. The Rockwood Depot and post office stood here until 1941. *Courtesy of Dorothy Lechner*

in 1891. The road crossed mountains to the northwest near the Purgatory-Durango Mountain ski area.

Rockwood was one of three horse-changing locations on the Animas Canyon Toll Road that connected Animas City and Silverton. The road was essential for delivering mail and supplies. The other two stops were at Cascade Hill, near Cascade Wye, and Ten Mile Creek.

The D&RG's construction crew set up a large camp in Rockwood while they worked on the line to Silverton. Work continued unabated through the winter of 1881-82 on

the most challenging portion of the line to Silverton, the High Line, and the nearby bridge over the Animas River.

The workers suffered from frigid temperatures that winter; there were many reported cases of frozen feet and fingers. Some of the laborers lived in caves that they dug into the hillside just south of the track — even with their families! Evidently, the caves offered more shelter than the thin-walled boxcars that the railroad had provided for the workers.

The climate here was great for growing russet potatoes, and lots of spuds were shipped up the tracks to

469

The Environment

The ecosystem from 7,000 to 9,000 feet elevation is called montane. Precipitation can be as high as 25 inches, but in southwest Colorado it is frequently less. The vegetation on south-facing slopes can be quite different than on adjacent, north-facing slopes. The montane region features a coniferous forest, often found on more moist northern slopes. Ponderosa pine, blue and Engelmann spruce, and Douglas fir are often dominant, interspersed with aspen, cottonwoods, and poplars. Montane areas are excellent habitat for birds.

Huge stands of Ponderosa pine in southwest Colorado were once considered some of the finest in the West, and supported a large timber industry that was aided by the railroad.

Typically, ponderosa pine dominates the lower range of the montane zone, but much of it has been logged around here. Ponderosa pine forests are difficult to reestablish: trees must be at least 25 years old to reproduce, they only produce large quantities of seeds every three to five years, and seeds only germinate in an unusually moist spring.

You have undoubtedly noticed a number of dead and dying trees around the region. The cause is an unprecedented attack of beetles here, and all across the Rockies. Pine beetles and different varieties of bark beetles are munching through piñon pines at lower elevations, and ponderosa, lodgepole, spruce, and fir at higher elevations. Trees have been weakened by the ongoing drought and have lost much of their natural resistance to beetle invasion. The problem is going to remain with us for ten years or so, until the little creatures finally eat themselves out of accessible forests.

Charismatic marmots are sometimes called *whistle pigs* because of the chirp or whistle they emit at the slightest provocation. Groundhogs, celebrated as weather predictors, are members of the marmot family.

The natural balance of things got thrown out of whack with the extensive logging of mature trees that took place during the past century, and the suppression of wildfires in many western forests. The congested growth of trees that replaced the old forests has enabled the beetles to spread easily from one tree to the next.

Wildlife you may spot between Rockwood and Silverton include black bears, big horn sheep, coyotes, beaver, porcupines, and an occasional moose.

This is a rare and rather primitive stub switch at the tail of the wye in Rockwood. It operates by actually bending both rails from one direction to another, which was possible only on the lighter narrow gauge rail.

On all switches, the red circle "target" indicates the switch is lined to the siding, while the green diamond shows the switch is set to the main track.

The rock cut you pass through at Rockwood was used by stuntmen in the movie "Butch Cassidy and the Sundance Kid" for the train robbery scene.

Years earlier, both sides were linked with papier-maché, to resemble a tunnel, for the film "Around the World in 80 Days!"

Silverton. Rockwood became a popular picnicking spot for Durangoans taking advantage of the convenient train transportation.

Today, Rockwood is still an important siding for the D&SNG. The railroad stores track-maintenance equipment and supplies here, and many passengers drive to Rockwood to board the train.

The old farm equipment dates back to the days when the Rockwood valley was an important agricultural area.

469

59

As you depart Rockwood, you are leaving behind most of the modern world. Until your train reaches Silverton there are no roads reaching into the Animas Canyon, and little has changed in appearance since the rail line was installed back in 1881-82.

469.2: Get your camera ready! Less than a half-mile from Rockwood you begin to cross the High Line, considered one of the most spectacular railroading views in the world.

470: A mineshaft dating from 1882 is visible here; it was part of an operation called Central Prospect that was never a large producer.

470.2: A long wooden trestle along the Overland Curve is visible in the early William Henry Jackson photograph shown on page 21. The structure was destroyed in 1904 when sparks from a passing locomotive ignited a blaze. Rather than re-installing another raised platform, the railroad decided to add fill to bring up the track level.

Between Rockwood and the High Bridge the tracks drop about 400 feet in elevation. This is the only

469.6: The train rides on a rock ledge, some 240 feet above the Animas River, that was created with extensive black powder blasting. To drill into the rock and set their charges, workers were lowered perilously over the granite cliffs in harnesses. Area miners were hired to do much of this work—a similar technique was used to dislodge ore in the mines. As far as we know, no workers died while working on the High Line.

The train on the opposite page is shown returning to Rockwood, coming around the tightest curve (28 degrees) on the D&SNG's 45-mile line. You may be able to hear wheels squeaking against the rails as the train negotiates the sharp turn.

469

470

471.23: The High Bridge is a favorite spot for photographers; while the locomotive is over the river, the fireman and engineer alternately open the "blowdown" valve to clear sediment that accumulates on the bottom of the boiler. The hot, white mist shoots dramatically from the sides of the locomotive, and on sunny days, rainbows can magically appear.

downgrade on the entire line from Durango to Silverton. From here north, once again, the grade is challenging.

471.23: The High Bridge, 190 feet long, is made of steel girders with a heavy wooden deck. In 1894, this bridge replaced the original all-timber trestle that had been constructed during the fall and winter of 1881-82. The current bridge was reinforced in 1981 to support the heavier K-36 series of locomotives (480s) that Charles Bradshaw Jr. wanted to use on the line. Up until then, the heaviest locomotives operating on the Silverton Branch were K-28s (470s).

472.05: Canyon Creek.

472.28: The hydroelectric Tacoma Power Plant was built in 1905, and began operations the following year. Two of the three generators at the plant are original.

Transformers originally intended for Tacoma, Washington were sent here with Tacoma Hydro Power stamped on the crates. The local supervisor thought the label referred to his power plant, and the name stuck. The first recipient of electricity from Tacoma was a mill in Silverton, and the town still receives power from here.

Water to power the generators flows 2 1/2 miles through a steel pipe from Electra Lake to a precipice 937 feet above the plant, where it free-falls to the power plant below.

471

471.8: December 21, 1921, was a sad day for the railroad: just east of Tacoma, a train powered by two engines and pulling a flanger (used to clear snow and ice from the tracks) struck some rocks; the two locomotives and the flanger went into the river. One of the firemen, John Connor, was killed and an engineer, Jim Connor (not related), spent six months in the hospital. The Colorado Railroad Museum

Where the man-made Electra Lake sits today, there were once eight lakes. The lake is fed by water from Cascade Creek, up by the landmark Engineer Mountain, through a system of open wooden flumes 10 feet in diameter. Until around 1930, there were 75 employees working on the flumes and the power plant.

472

Tacoma is capable of producing eight megawatts of electricity per hour, enough to supply 8,000 homes. Currently there are studies underway by the current owner, the large Colorado utility Xcel, to consider adding a new, more efficient generator to the plant.

The only access to the power plant, that requires year-round supervision, is the railroad line. Tacoma has its own gas-powered track car to transport employees over the rails.

474: "Ah! Wilderness" was a dude ranch that operated from 1952 until 1985. Kids on ponies used to "race"

474.65: Tank Creek water tank is the first of two watering stops for the train on its way north to Silverton. After the train's long push from Durango, the tender is almost depleted and will require as much as 4,500 gallons of water! The engine crew normally "oils around" and inspects the locomotive at this stop.

The original wooden water tank here was removed in 1966 and has been replaced by a recycled tank off of a railroad tank car.

Above the tank, not visible from the train, is a solid concrete dam that the D&SNG's maintenance of way crew built to ensure a reliable supply of running water for the train throughout the year.

When concrete pours are needed, batch trucks are ramped up onto railroad flatcars and hauled by a locomotive out to the construction site.

the train when it came by. Today the buildings of the old facility are used to house employees of the nearby Tall Timber Resort.

The large meadow here is one of the locations used by the railroad during the annual Photographer's Special that takes place each fall.

475.25: Tall Timber is a luxury resort that has received the prestigious Mobil 4-Star rating. The facility is accessible only by rail or Tall Timber's own helicopter service that also helps with local search and rescue operations. A small golf course

is on part of the meadow grounds. A new system of tree-soaring platforms, to the east of the tracks, has been installed for thrill seekers.

476.15: Grasshopper Creek Bridge.

476.7: A retaining wall known as "cement fill" was built here after the 1970 flood to help divert water away from the roadbed.

476.9: Little Cascade Creek.

477.00: In January, 1916, a D&RG train faced with heavy snowdrifts stopped here. The locomotive

477

475: In the meadow located at today's Tall Timber Resort, an actual train wreck was once enacted for the movie "Denver and Rio Grande." Two old loco motives, 319 and 345 (that one disguised as 268), were sacrificed for the occasion; they were first loaded with dynamite and black powder to bolster the explosion. The crews on each locomotive opened the throttles and jumped off. The collision created more of a blast than had been anticipated, and it was lucky that no spectators were injured.

The thunderous explosion resulted in such a huge amount of debris that for years the site was referred to as "Scrap Iron Junction."

D&RGW President Wilson McCarthy viewed the spectacular crash and afterwards said: "This is a helluva way to run a railroad!"

Edmond O'Brien is shown protecting Laura Elliot from the bad guys in a publicity still from the 1952 Hollywood production "Denver & Rio Grande," a time when American audiences were captivated by the genre of Western movies.   The Allan C. Lewis Collection

475

477.55: Cascade Canyon Wye was built in 1981, and permits turning of the Cascade Canyon Winter Train. A 2,400-square foot structure called Cascade Station is used as a lunch area for the winter train, and the facility is available for private parties other times of the year.

Photo by Yvonne Lashmett

uncoupled from the coaches to plow snow off the tracks. Intuitive passengers left on board realized that they were in a precarious spot; they abandoned the passenger car and moved a short distance away. Soon afterwards, a snow slide came down that totally buried the coach!

Today's winter train avoids most of the heavy avalanches that occur further up the Animas Canyon to the north, but there are potential problems running the train in heavy-snow years, even to Cascade Canyon Wye. A bulldozer is sometimes kept near MP 477 to keep rails clear.

477.55: Cascade Canyon, west of the tracks. Cascade Creek meets the

Animas River just north of the 16-car wye. Tracing Cascade Creek's drainage uphill to the west, you find the confluence of Lime Creek in an area known as Purgatory Flats. The huge Lime Creek burn of June 1879 started near the Animas River and roared up these drainages, scorching over 26,000 acres from Spud Mountain to Molas Pass. Effects of the blaze are still obvious today, showing how slowly vegetation recovers at these high elevations.

The cause of the fire has never been determined, but at the time, it was widely believed that Ute Indians started the blaze, protesting unfair treatment after the Brunot Treaty of 1873.

477

67

477.9: An interesting artifact located near Tefft spur is the abandoned boiler of Otto Mears' Silverton, Gladstone & Northerly's locomotive #32, named the Gold King, shown in this photo.

The boiler, which could have been fired with wood or coal, was used to power machinery at the saw mill here. Mears sacrificed his locomotive in the re-building effort of the Silverton Branch and his own lines out of Silverton, after the destructive flood of October 1911, when thousands of railroad ties were washed downstream.   The D&SNGRR

477.80: Tracks cross the Animas River over the steel-trussed Tefft Bridge. The Purgatory hiking trail, which starts at Highway 550 near Durango Mountain Resort, crosses the tracks here and continues north for another seven miles to Needleton.

477.9: The old Tefft Spur, named for an early forest ranger, Guy Tefft.

This was the site of a large sawmill that operated in the 1890s and supplied railroad ties for the Silverton Northern Railroad. Obviously, the location of the site was convenient for loading the ties on flat cars.

Although the records are not totally clear, it appears that the sawmill was acquired by Otto Mears after he took control of the Silverton, Gladstone, & Northerly Railroad around 1910 or 1911. On October 5, 1911, the worst flooding in Colorado history did extensive damage to Mears' lines out of Silverton as well as to the D&RG's Silverton Branch. Mears oversaw the rebuild-

477

ing of all the lines, and afterwards went into semi-retirement, turning over his railroad business to his son-in-law, James R. Pitcher.

The Animas Canyon Toll Road that preceded the railroad through the canyon by five years, passed through Tefft, known then as Niccora. A post office operated here for just over four months, from July 16, 1877 until November 26 of that same year. The postmaster, Thomas

Blackledge, then left for the winter, never to return.

478.30: A portion of the old Animas Canyon Toll Road is discernible, going uphill on the west side of the tracks.

478.44: The old Cascade siding.

479.55: The Bitter Root Mine/ Bowen's Ranch. William and Jane Bowen of Silverton established a

478.44: The D&SNG helped the Colorado Division of Wildlife re-introduce Rocky Mountain Bighorn Sheep to the upper Animas Canyon on a snowy January 27, 2001. The sheep had been captured the day before near Georgetown, Colorado, then put into trailers and driven to a waiting boxcar in Rockwood.

When the boxcar doors were opened, the sheep were tentative for a few moments, and then they bolted! Another boxcar load of sheep was released the following year. The sheep have adjusted well to their new environment and are sometimes spotted near the tracks.

This was also the location of the old Cascade Siding, not to be confused with today's Cascade Canyon Wye. The siding has been used for loading livestock and was once the site of a section house.

478

479.55: The D&RG once placed telephone booths like this one, located along the tracks at Schaaf's cabin, throughout their system. Other phones on the Silverton Branch were located at Rockwood and Elk Park.

Durango resident and train afficionado Bruce Anderson, pictured here, put the new roof and fresh paint on this phone booth during the summer of 2001. In 2006, Bruce helped paint the nearby house.

Long before the era of two-way radios, section crews would use the phones to communicate anything noteworthy to the railroad. In the early years, section crews were in charge of inspecting and maintaining a seven-mile "section" of the line and the D&RG sometimes built section houses in remote areas.

ranch and way station here along the old Animas Canyon Toll Road. The remains of the Bitter Root Mine, named for the former Montana home of Oscar Schaff's wife, are visible just south of the meadow. The two cabins here were originally built as D&RG railroad buildings at Cascade siding and were moved here.

480.6: Pajarito, meaning small bird in Spanish, is the site of a small spring just west of the tracks. A favorite stop for track patrolmen, the spring flows during the driest of times and has delicious tasting water. Remnants of a log cabin, probably used by miners, can be seen to the east, between the tracks and the river.

481.5: Government Bridge.

482.31: The original Needleton station. Before the railroad arrived, this had been a stop on the Animas Canyon Toll Road. A post office operated here from 1882 until January 1910. The area had been combed for gold as early as the 1860s, and Needleton supplied

478

479.5: Pigeon, Turret, and Eolus Peaks, from left, loom above the Photographer's Special Train, September 2001. The Needles Range is visible from several vantage points along the line.

The Bitter Root Mine, located up the hillside to the west here, as well as some placer claims along the river, were operated by Oscar Schaaf. Schaaf's cabin and the house of a former fire warden are situated in the small meadow here.

prospectors heading up Needle Creek and into the Chicago Basin. Significant mining activity occurred along these slopes, but none of the mines were ever very productive. Mining continued sporadically in the Chicago Basin until the area was designated part of the Weminuche Wilderness in 1975. Flooding in 1927 washed away most of the original Needleton town site.

482.50: The Needleton Slide, followed by the Hunt Slide at 482.80,

both run down the steep slopes west of the tracks. These are the first snow slides north of Cascade Canyon Wye that maintenance of way crews expect to clear before the train starts running to Silverton in the spring. In 1993, the Hunt Slide covered the tracks with over 80 feet of snow. Snow slides occur frequently between here and Silverton in the steep gullies that drain into the Animas Canyon. You may notice stunted trees and vegetation on the upper slopes, marking sites where

482

483.7: This derailment took place in July 1951, when crews for the D&RGW were hurrying to accommodate the filming of the crash scene in the movie *Denver & Rio Grande* shown on page 66. Locomotive 473 hit a "heat kink" in the tracks and jack-knifed. Fireman M. Rhodes, a practicing preacher, was caught in the squeeze between the locomotive and the tender, and narrowly escaped being killed. The curve here is now named for the engineer on that train, John Dieckman. The D&SNGRR.

avalanches periodically mow them over.

483.30: The Needleton flag stop is adjacent to the popular trailhead to Chicago Basin. On the east side of the river are some private cabins on old mining claims.

484: The Needleton siding.

484.4: Site of the original tank that was built in 1881 and was cosmetically restored between 2003-04. The currently used tankcar-tank, set in the 1960s, receives gravity-fed water from Watertank Creek, as did the original tank.

483 484.60: Ruby Creek.

485.40: No Name Creek enters the Animas from the east.

485.70: Mountain View Crest and No Name Slide. No Name Rapids, a dangerous, thrilling stretch of class 5 whitewater is just upriver from here.

486.60: Mud Slide closed the railroad in 1986, and again, during Railfest in 1999, because of a massive 20-foot wall of debris that came down during heavy rains.

487.10 – 488: Though not indicated on the elevation profile, page 75, this is the steepest grade on the entire line—up to 4%! After filling the tender with water at Needleton,

484.4: The original Needleton water tank was a stop for the train on the way to Silverton until the mid-1970s. As you can see, it was becoming quite dilapidated. A restoration project headed by Fritz Klinke of Silverton, and funded by the state of Colorado Historical Fund, returned the tank to its original appearance, completing the work in 2004.

Though the tank does not hold water, the structure is stabilized and could be adapted at some point in the future. Water is dispensed from the body of a steel tank car just north of the wooden tank at MP 484.5.

487

485.5: Sculpted rock here in the Animas River is known as "Ten Mile Granite." Although the waters of the Animas continue to erode the rock, most of the shaping was done by glaciers.
The rocks create "No Name Rapids," popular with rafters and kayakers.

the fireman must work hard to get the boiler to full steaming temperature for this tough stretch.

487.15: Ten Mile Creek is exactly ten miles from Silverton. It was named by Animas Canyon Toll Road builders in the 1870s and was a stop on the road to change horses. Ten Mile House stood nearby; during the 1880s, the owner of Ten Mile House, Franz Schneider, was sometimes asked to deliver mail and critical supplies via sled and dogteam to snowbound Silverton when the tracks were impassable for the train.

487.5: Garfield Slide is the site of multiple avalanches that continue for a half-mile down the steep west face of Mount Garfield and across

the river, sometimes blocking the tracks with a huge volume of snow and debris.

488.4: Red Young Slide also descends from Mount Garfield. It was named for an engineer who lost his life when the train he was piloting slammed into a rockslide here in 1897. Avalanches are common here.

489.60: This is an area where avalanches from the east sometimes dam the river, creating what maintenance of way crews call Coleman Lake. In the spring, water draining from the slide has repeatedly roared over the rails, washing out the roadbed. The spot is named for the unfortunate equipment operator whose bulldozer got buried in the muck until the waters receded.

487

489.87: Fifty-five foot Elk Park Bridge, in the foreground, was installed over the Animas in the late fall of 1964. Periodic flooding had seriously weakened the abutments of the old trestle seen here, just to the west.

The D&SNG offers access to mountains that are in the heart of the San Juans. Hikers save a great amount of time reaching the magnificent peaks of the Needles Range and the Grenadiers, shown below from Molas Lake, by following trails that lead from train stops in Needleton and Elk Park.

489

75

490.7: Elk Park is dominated by Mount Garfield. Trainmen sometimes call the landmark Gorilla Mountain. Do you see a resemblance to King Kong's profile facing the tracks near the top of the peak?

In this upper portion of the Animas River, rocks have a reddish tint from the oxidation of minerals that have leached into the water from hundreds of nearby abandoned mines and mill tailings ponds. The river is gradually being returned to health through reclamation efforts of federal and state governments and local organizations, notably the Animas River Stakeholders Group. Trout are gradually moving upstream to areas of the river that only a few years ago were unable to sustain them. The portion of the Animas River that runs through Durango was once as discolored as what you see here.

489.90: Animas River bridges.

490.10: The Minco uranium mine has a small spur and loading dock west of the tracks here. The owners periodically work the operation to keep their mining claim active.

490.20: Elk Creek.

489

76

490.70: Elk Park is a beautiful and historic site. In 1884, a wye was built here to enable trains blocked by the deep snow slides further north to turn around, and it was used for this purpose until the 1950s. Animal-powered pack trains would continue transporting supplies to Silverton from here when possible. There was also a D&RG section house here at one time.

Stock-loading facilities were built in Elk Park for the herds of sheep that the railroad brought up to access summer pastures.

Today Elk Park is well known to outdoor enthusiasts seeking a convenient approach to the Grenadiers and beyond.

491.25: The footbridge across the Animas River near Molas Creek is part of the Colorado Trail system that connects Denver to Durango.

491.30: Molas Creek.

491.95: Whitehead Creek (Gulch).

492.5: Snowshed Slide got its name from a massive log structure that was built in 1890 to divert two avalanches that would converge on the tracks here. Made of heavy timbers, the snowshed performed well until the D&RGW tore it down in 1949 when the framework needed extensive repairs. Locomotives had become larger and more powerful by then and it was thought they could push through most snow slides. Winter trains to Silverton were also becoming infrequent then.

The Snowshed Slide area frequently needs clearing in the spring to

The unusual and photogenic Colorado Blue Columbine is the state flower. *Columbine* comes from a latin word meaning "dove-like." The flower is common in the high country of Colorado during the warmest months of summer.

492

492.50: Snowshed Slide is the largest avalanche on the Silverton Branch. The rare old photograph above shows the snowshed soon after its construction in 1890. Obviously, the D&RG went to great lengths attempting to maintain access to Silverton. The Allan C. Lewis Collection
   Below, a work train being used in the snow-clearing effort at Snowshed Slide in the spring of 2005 is dwarfed by the slide that almost totally obscures the Animas River.

enable the first trains of the season to get to Silverton. During years of heavy snowfall, as during 1993 and 2005, the slide runs all the way across the river, approximately 120 feet deep! Hard-working MOW crews have always responded to the challenge, clearing the way for the first scheduled run to Silverton in early May.

493.60: Twin Sisters Slide.

494.00: Cleveland Slide.

494.20: The Deer Park Creek water tank was built here and served the railroad until it was destroyed by a snow slide in the early 1920s. Still visible are the tank's delivery pipe and concrete foundation.

492

495.25: The Silverton Bridge, also known to trainmen as the Timber Bridge, marks the train's last crossing of the Animas River before entering Silverton. Although it has been structurally maintained, the bridge is relatively unchanged in appearance since its installation in 1882.

At this point, the river drainage encompasses about 4,000,000 acres of the upper San Juans.

494.60: Remains of a tipple used by the King Mine to fill ore cars on a small spur can be seen here. Kendall Falls comes cascading down from hundreds of feet above, just north of the old tipple. The mine lay in Cataract Gulch, on the west side of the river, and ore was cabled across, powered by an old locomotive tank that you can see from the east side of the train. The cascades on the west side of the river are known to railroaders as Angel Veil Falls.

494.62: Kendall Creek.

494.70: Cataract Canyon (The Narrows).

495.10: Deadwood Gulch descends from Grand Turk Mountain to the

west, and looking up, you can see evidence of the old Detroit Mine. The hill just above the river has always been a favorite picnicking spot for Silverton residents. Deadwood Falls adds to the ambiance.

495.25: As your train crosses the Animas River for the last time, you

495

are entering the broad, rocky valley historically known as Baker's Park, named for Charles Baker, who led a prospecting party here in 1860.

The large operation that you see just west of the tracks was part of the Pittsberg Mines that operated here through the 1980s. The area at one time had its own railroad spur.

496.15: Mineral Creek girder-bridge.

496.30: The Silverton Wye is used to turn your train around during your brief stay in town. If their loco-motive had any trouble steaming (or breathing) on the way up, engine

crews will use this area to "shake the grates" of the firebox and dump out coal ash, shale, and *klinkers*. Klinkers are unburned pieces of coal that melt and fuse together.

496.70: The Silverton Depot served as the terminus of the D&RG line for many years. A big welcoming celebration for the arrival of the D&RG here in July 1882 was a little premature. Festivities were planned for the Fourth of July, and indeed a celebration did occur, but the guest of honor was not present. Construction crews were still laying down rails a couple of miles from town, and the first train did not arrive in Silverton until July 8. By

The stem of this wye, used to change the direction of your train, once connected to the old Silverton Railroad line that continued to the mining town of Albany, in Ironton Park, 18 miles to the north. Read about the Silverton Railroad in the Otto Mears section, page 102.

495

80

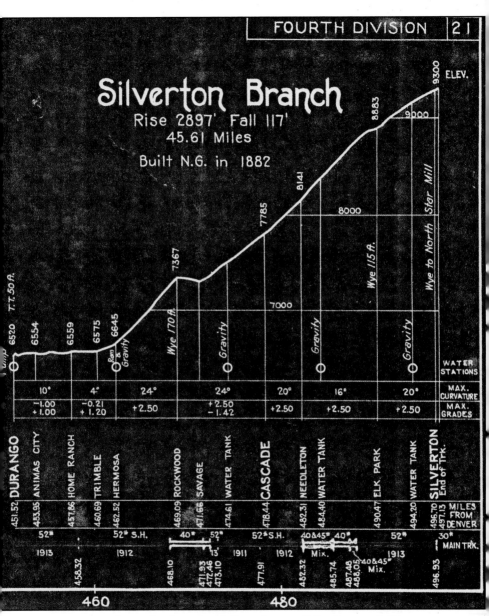

Silverton Branch
Rise 2897' Fall 117'
45.61 Miles
Built N.G. in 1882

This elevation profile done by civil engineers of the Denver & Rio Grande graphically shows the gradient between Durango and Silverton, the maximum degree of curvature between points, and the location of water tanks.

496

that time, miners had gone back to work, and there was not a great amount of fanfare to greet the train. The railroad got busy too; the first passenger train left Silverton on July 11, and the first ore was hauled to Durango two days later.

The Silverton Depot was built in 1882 as a temporary structure because the townspeople and the D&RG could not agree on a suitable permanent location for the building. (Some current Silverton residents observe that if they were trying to agree on a site today, the two parties would probably still have a hard time agreeing!) The same "temporary" building is still standing today.

The D&RGW donated the depot to the San Juan Historical Society in 1969, and that organization made repairs to the building. For seven years the depot was leased to the well-known purveyor of historic books, Sundance Publications, as a printing facility and office. In 1985, the D&SNG re-acquired the building, and it has functioned for the

On Friday, September 12, 1975, the Silverton Depot was badly damaged by an explosion that occurred just before the arrival of a train. Grate-fully, no lives were lost.

The blast did extensive damage to the south end of the building, and was triggered by a fuse that burned for only about seven minutes. That left little time for the perpetrator to escape, but escape he did. Despite the largest criminal investigation in San Juan County history, no one has ever been charged with the crime and no motives are known.

496

The Allan C. Lewis Collection

Lynn Hutson, Silverton Stationmaster.

railroad ever since. The Silverton Depot and Freight Yard Museum were opened to the public in 1999.

You can get a real feel for mountain-railroading looking over the display at the Silverton Freight Yard Museum: outfit cars, some equipped with kitchen facilities, were used to house crews when they were on duty away from home. Side-dump gondolas (gondola, by the way, describes any open-topped freight car) served a purpose at each end of the Silverton Branch: leaving here, they were filled with ore from local

The area around the Silverton Depot is pretty tranquil these days, but it was once the hub of a huge amount of activity. Close to the Depot was a small roundhouse, section house, coal shed, and other railroading facilities. Feed, coal, lumber, and hardware businesses that utilized the railroads all had facilities close by.

In the early 1900s, Silverton was served by four railroads, making it, at the time, the town with the most railroads at its service in the U.S.

496

Enjoy the pleasure of breathing in mountain air around Silverton! The EPA monitors air quality on nearby Molas Pass, and it ranks as some of the most pristine in North America.

mines bound for the Durango smelter. On their return, the gondolas often brought coal to fuel the many heating stoves in Silverton.

Old locomotive #493 was originally built for the D&RGW as standard gauge engine. Two old tank cars that used to sit in the Silverton Yard, and formerly carried oil out of the San Juan Basin near Farmington, have been converted to water cars by the D&SNG, to aid in fire-fighting efforts.

Today the Silverton Depot functions much as it always has for the railroad. The station agent sells tickets to the public and is a source for train information. The depot is also a communication center and shelter for train employees.

The track set-offs at the depot are used as resting spots for D&SNG patrol cars out of the train's way.

496.90: 12th Street and Blair marks the end of the line for the D&SNG in Silverton. Most of the activity in town is located within a short walk from here.

Remember the elevation in Silverton is a lofty 9,300 feet, so take it easy, and drink lots of water to avoid dehydration

496

The Environment

The region around Silverton from 9,000 feet to treeline is classified as sub-alpine forest. Precipitation here averages over 30 inches a year, much of it snow, making this area one of the most hydrated areas in Colorado. The San Juans are a watershed for a large area of southwest Colorado and New Mexico. Summers can be cool, a respite from hot southwest weather, with spells of monsoonal afternoon and evening thunderstorms.

Columbine, Engelman spruce, Douglas fir, and white fir are common in this region. Spruce-fir forests dominate where they have enough moisture. These trees have short needles allowing them to shed snow easily, and because they grow close together they buffer the wind. The long cold winters here keep this ecosystem from being very diverse. Sunshine is intense here with the thinner atmosphere. Be sure to wear sunscreen.

Alpine tundra is found above tree line, which usually starts around 12,000 feet. Alpine tundra receives significant snowfall, but much of it is blown down to lower elevations, creating a very harsh, dry environment with meager topsoil that supports only mosses and lichens. There are many reminders in the high mining areas around Silverton that once this delicate environment is disturbed, it takes decades to regenerate.

Little Molas Lake, elevation 11,000 feet.

Silverton, the Heart of a Mining Empire

It was not until 1860 that the valley pictured above drew the attention of newly arrived prospectors to Colorado. For at least three centuries before then, the San Juan Range in remote southwestern Colorado had been the seasonal domain of Ute hunting parties but remained largely unexplored by Anglo-Europeans. Brief incursions by Spanish explorers seeking gold had already given much of the surrounding area Spanish names before 1776, when missionaries Escalante and Dominguez trekked through the San Juans just north of here, searching for a new route from Santa Fe to missions in northern California.

Rumors of gold and silver in the San Juans preceded a disastrous venture into the region by a U. S. government party headed by John C. Fremont in the autumn of 1848. Eleven members of his 33-man

The D&SNGRR; photo by W. H. Jackson

group perished in the mountains that winter. A lone member of Fremont's party reportedly discovered placer gold along a tributary to the San Juan River, close to Pagosa Springs, but kept his discovery a secret. When he returned to stake his claim the following year, the unfortunate fellow was unable to relocate his discovery.

In the summer of 1860, Captain Charles Baker led a party of prospectors who had gathered in Oro City—near present day Leadville—into the San Juans and the valley that would soon become known as Baker's Park. Exaggerated tales of gold and silver that circulated through the newly established mining camps in Colorado lured Baker and his group to the San Juans, even though most of the territory there belonged to sometimes hostile Ute Indians.

The prospecting team scoured the region looking for evidence of easy-to-pan placer gold in the Animas River and its tributaries. While there was no large find, they did find traces of gold and some promising veins. Actual mining production was delayed, though; the group's supplies were dwindling, and they faced the threat of Ute hostilities—several prospectors reportedly lost their lives that year. Baker and his party retreated from the high San Juans down to the Animas Valley using a trail along Lime Creek—the same route the Utes followed to reach their summer hunting grounds.

News of the impending American Civil War caused Baker, who joined Confederate forces, and his men to reconsider their mining aspirations, and they disbanded. The San Juans were again left to the Utes, as most prospecting activity ceased in the region while the war raged. The end of the Civil War in 1865 marked the beginning of a huge migration of settlers to the American West. News of Baker's findings before the war had persisted around Colorado, and prospectors started to trickle back into the San Juans.

The first organized mining activi-

Pack trains, like this one on Silverton's Greene Street, supplied miners with the great quantities of equipment they needed in the remote reaches of the San Juans. In the effort, tens of thousands of mules, horses, and oxen were driven over the region's rough, narrow roads. The wide streets in Silverton were designed to enable a pack train to turn around easily. An elevated bandstand is visible down the street.

ty in the Silverton area came in 1870, when a gold claim was staked at the Little Giant Lode in Arrastra Gulch. Despite the crude type of processing that was then available, the ore yielded an encouraging $150 per ton. When word of the successful stake spread, increasing numbers of prospectors headed into the San Juans, although the Ute "problem" was still unresolved and the prospectors were all trespassing. Sporadic violence between the two groups continued, and Charles Baker was killed, in 1871, by Indians somewhere near the Park that bears his name.

In 1868, the Utes had signed an agreement with the U.S. Government that gave them sovereignty over most of Colorado west of the Continental Divide, including, of course, the San Juan region. But that was before the promise of gold and silver in the San Juans had gained much attention. By the early 1870s, ever-increasing numbers of miners with the "fever" headed for the San Juans, though, legally, they were violating the 1868 treaty. With title to the land in the hands of the Utes, miners could not have legal title to their claims. They demanded government intervention; the often-heard refrain was "The Utes must go!"

The Utes are a tribe that has lived in both the plains and mountains of Colorado longer than any other cultural group – hundreds, if not thousands of years. When faced with the

The spectacular 4th of July celebration in Silverton has roots back to the old days, when it was one of the year's only two paydays for area miners.

increasing waves of European immigrants, they attempted a policy of peaceful co-existence. The leading proponent of that philosophy among the Utes was Chief Ouray, who was largely responsible for maintaining mostly peaceful relations between Utes and the new settlers. Bitterness among the Utes was understandable. They had already been moved off much of their land and had received very little in return.

Chief Ouray had no illusions about dealing with U.S officials. In

In the summer of 2001, carpenters re-assembled the Caledonia boarding house that was moved from Minnie Gulch. It has now become part of the town's new mining museum that opened in May, 2006. Silverton has received numerous grants in recent years to renovate some of the area's finest remaining structures.

the midst of negotiations in 1868 he said "The agreement an Indian makes to a United States treaty is like the agreement a buffalo makes with his hunter when pierced with arrows. All he can do is lie down and give in."

By the early 1870s, it was clear that a new arrangement between the Utes and the U.S. was needed to prevent an escalation of violence in the San Juans. Otto Mears, who would soon be building railroads in the area, and Chief Ouray were the key figures in negotiations that began in 1872, and resulted in the Brunot Treaty, signed in 1873. In this agreement, the Utes ceded claim to four million acres of the most prized mining area in the San Juans. In return, the Utes were to be guaranteed hunting rights in the lower elevations, financial compensation, and safe reservations. Miners

welcomed the Brunot Treaty, but there was confusion between them and the Utes over the boundaries of the hunting land, and that continued to be a source of friction.

With the signing of the Brunot Treaty, the San Juans were legally opened for mining and the boom was on! A prospector with his pack animal became a common sight throughout the region. Two men from the original Baker party were among the first to return to Baker's Park.

The U. S. Treasury used gold and silver at this time, so demand for both minerals was high. Within a year, more than 1,500 mining claims had been staked in the San Juans.

Silverton began the classic Western "boomtown" experience. By the fall of 1874, the population in and around Silverton had swollen to 4,000 people, and there were over

This is a view of the Animas valley above Silverton, looking in the direction of the Sunnyside Mine, in Eureka and Animas Forks. The town of Howardsville, the county seat before Silverton, used to be right across the river here.

100, mostly wood frame, buildings in Silverton, including a schoolhouse.

Silverton had postal service before it had a post office; the first appointed postmaster, Jacob M. Hanks, hand-delivered mail out of his hip pocket while waiting for his post office to be finished.

Numerous newspapers have served Silverton. The La Plata Miner was established in 1875, and later combined with The Silverton Standard, forming The Silverton Standard and Miner. Still operating today, it is the oldest continuously running business and newspaper in Colorado.

George Greene opened the first smelter in the San Juans in 1875, but there was not enough coal

around Silverton to make it work efficiently and the operation folded as soon as the D&RG started shipping ore to the Durango smelter.

For a time, Silverton boasted having one of the state's largest breweries. The owner of the brewery, Charles Fischer, advertised his beer as a tonic, not as an intoxicant.

Silverton did have competition for supremacy in the mining region of the San Juans. Howardsville, located at the base of Stony Pass and Cunningham Gulch, was the first attempted settlement in the original La Plata County. Named for George W. Howard, who encouraged passersby to help him hoist logs up on his new cabin by offering them a swig of whiskey, Howardsville was the county seat before

Silverton. In 1876, voters elected to move the seat to Silverton where it has remained ever since. Howardsville today is a ghost town with only a few original buildings still standing. The town of Red Mountain was a thriving mining community until fires destroyed most of its buildings in 1893, and again in 1895; the town was never able to recover.

According to legend, the name Silverton was not derived from the commonly assumed abbreviation of "silver town." Reportedly, the name was created when a miner was asked whether there was much gold in the area; his response: "We ain't found any gold but we struck that blasted silver by the hunnerd ton!"

The year of 1876 was important to the area in several ways: Colorado became the nation's 38th state, Silverton became an incorporated town, and most importantly to southwest Colorado, the D&RG announced its intention to build a line to Silverton.

Up until that point, the greatest deterrent to growth in Silverton remained its severe isolation and the lack of dependable, affordable transportation. The most frequently used route for travel over Stony Pass was difficult at best. The D&RG was the answer to the dilemma, and it is impossible to overestimate the

A storm clears on a crisp fall day in Silverton. The Grand Imperial Hotel, in the foreground, was built in 1883, by W. S. Thomson of England. It was considered the social center during the early years of mining here.

Though the mines are no longer active around Silverton, they survive in spirit. Every summer, locals and miners from all over the country gather at Hardrocker's Holidays to celebrate mining's contributions to the area and to test their skills and strength, as exemplified in the hard fought tug-of-war shown above.

impact of the railroad's arrival in Silverton in 1882.

With a reliable rail system and silver prices high, the area thrived. It is said that mining in the San Juans produced more millionaires than anywhere else in the country during this era. The period of prosperity was to continue for the next 30 years, with one notable exception, during the Silver Panic in 1893.

Mining fortunes have always been subject to the roller coaster of worldwide economic demands and governmental policies. The U.S. Congress had propped up silver artificially in 1890 with the Sherman Silver Purchase Act and decided to withdraw that support in 1893. The dramatic drop in silver prices that resulted had a devastating impact on Silverton and mining activity throughout the region. In Silverton

alone, at least ten mines were closed and over 1,000 miners laid off. Recovery was slow, but Silverton was able to rebound because its mines had adequate amounts of gold and other base minerals to offset the drop in silver prices.

When the D&RG arrived in Silverton, they were unable to set the terms in negotiations with town officials as they had in Animas City several years earlier. Because of the way the valley was situated, the railroad had no alternate spot to set up operations, and the D&RG was forced to pay boomtown prices for the land it needed in Silverton.

The colorful cast of characters arriving in Silverton included those seeking, and offering, diversions to lonely miners. The red-light district along Blair Street, close to the present day train stop of the D&SNG, was considered as wild as any in

Colorado, featuring gambling, prostitution, and saloons that stayed open 24 hours a day.

During the 1890s, temperate members of Silverton society hired the renowned, dapper Bat Masterson and his gun-slinging gang to clean things up. Their efforts had little long-lasting impact. Mining was a masculine, often solitary, occupation, and many felt that the enterprises on Blair Street served an important social function for men seeking release from the tedium and danger of their jobs.

As in Durango, houses of prostitution and their employees had taxes levied on them, revenue that served the community at large. The last of the bordellos on Blair Street remained open until the 1950s.

There were other, healthier, social activities. Silverton was home to a nationally known band that was organized in the late 1880s. They were known as The Original Dodge City Cowboy Band, though they weren't really cowboys and were definitely from Silverton. The band attended ceremonies in Denver for two Colorado governors and traveled to Washington for the inauguration of President Benjamin Harrison.

Horseracing, boxing, baseball, and mining holidays were also popular activities. Durango's baseball team prevailed over Silverton's in a game played July 4, 1881, before the rail line was finished. With many sports, gambling and drinking were important parts of the attraction.

In those days, fire departments in

The Silverton Hillside cemetery, with the town in the valley below; of the more than 3,000 burials that have been documented here, at least 2,000 no longer have markers.

Most of the missing grave markers were made of wood and have completely deteriorated.

94

Civic pride and promotion were combined in this billboard that stood by the road into Silverton during the 1950s.

mining communities like Silverton, Ouray, and Telluride frequently competed to show off their prowess. The Reese Hook and Ladder Company of Silverton was renowned throughout the San Juans. The arrival of their truck over Stony Pass was cause for a great community celebration.

Most of the immigrants to Silverton were not attracted by its notoriety, they were lured by the potential to further themselves economically. They came from all over the world, but mostly from Europe: Italy, Germany, Scandinavia, Great Britain (especially from mining areas in Wales and Cornwall), and Ireland.

Significant numbers of Chinese were also present in Silverton for a time. Many of them had been introduced to this country while working on railroad projects in California. In a shameful episode of racism, hard-working Chinese were run out of Silverton en masse, for no apparent provocation, in 1902, never to return. The Chinese had never even been allowed gravesites in the local cemetery.

Many of the miners in Silverton had steady work and wanted to stay and have families, though men far outnumbered women here. The railroad's presence in Silverton had a civilizing influence. With safe, dependable transportation, respectable women were able to travel to Silverton, and the town

95

The impressive San Juan County Courthouse, built in 1907, at a cost of $79,000, is prominent in this photograph of Silverton taken from above Cement Creek. The Courthouse features a gold-colored dome and a clock tower. Snow-capped Snowden Peak lies in the background at 13,077 feet.

soon became a good place to raise a family, as it still is.

The D&RG was just one of four narrow gauge lines that served Silverton. The Silverton Railroad, the Silverton Northern, and the Silverton, Gladstone & Northerly were other lines that were built by Otto Mears to serve the mines, and they all connected with the D&RG

in Silverton.

From 1900 to 1912, mining was at its peak and the population of San Juan County reached 5,000. Silverton's finest public buildings, including the San Juan County Courthouse, the Silverton Town Hall, the Miners' Union Hospital, and the Carnegie Library all date from this period, reflecting an ornate, sophisticated style known as Victorian. The main business section of Silverton has survived basically intact since that era because its buildings have been spared the major fires that devastated other Colorado mining towns like Cripple Creek, Leadville, and Creede.

There was also an economic component to the old town's preservation. While the rest of the nation prospered during the 1920s through the 1950s, Silverton saw its fortunes diminish, as persistent low mineral prices forced many large mining operations to close down. Throughout the nation, in a push to modernize, many fine old buildings were abandoned and torn down, replaced by simple, nondescript structures. In Silverton, thankfully, there was not enough money around to invest in new construction and the wonderful old Victorian-style buildings remained. This set the stage for the development of tourism here, starting in the late 1940s.

In the fall of 1918, Silverton, along with much of the world, experienced a deadly bout with an epi-

Lunchtime entertainment in the Grand Imperial Hotel is provided by Durango native Lacey Black, playing an appropriately vintage piano.

demic of Spanish influenza (a misnomer because the outbreak really began in the Midwestern United States). People living at higher elevations seemed at greater risk of catching the disease, and Silverton was hit especially hard. During a six-week period in October and November, Silverton lost about ten percent of its population—150 people—one of the highest percentages in the country.

Gravediggers in Silverton could not keep up with the fatalities and two "flu trenches" were dug for 90 mass burials. Fear and suspicion gripped the area during the epidemic; some people who were healthy

The Silverton Brass Band has been in existence since 1976, and most agree that they are sounding better than ever today. Silverton hosts the annual Great Western Rocky Mountain Brass Festival that attracts musicians following in the tradition of John Philip Sousa, from near and far.

enough tried to leave Silverton but were turned away at Ouray by armed patrols.

Uncharacteristically, this strain of flu attacked many healthy, young adults. The population of Silverton was near its peak in 1918, and some say the town has never rebounded from the impact of the deadly virus.

The era of Prohibition, making the manufacture of intoxicating liquor illegal, started nationwide in 1920. It was one of the most violated laws in American history, but government enforcers known as "revenuers" shut down many illegal operations.

Silverton certainly had its share of stills and small breweries, but the perpetrators here had a unique advantage. Law enforcement officials had no way to reach Silverton except by train, since roads were so primitive at that time. That gave ample time for sympathetic Durangoans to warn violators in Silverton that trouble was on the way, allowing them to clean up their act.

The working class has shaped the character of Silverton. Union representation was widespread from the turn of the century and extended into businesses other than the mining industry, like newspapers and restaurants. A bond between blue-collar workers existed here long before the Great Depression and the

The Silverton Military Band, sponsored by the fraternal organization Woodmen of the World, was one of several bands in Silverton during the late 1800s. The Silverton Democrat, on February 19, 1887, stated: "...no town in [Colorado] of the same size has so much musical ability among its inhabitants."

The San Juan County Historical Society

implementation of the New Deal, and unions served as a safeguard to the community of Silverton. The UMWA (United Mine Workers) built the only hospital Silverton ever had during the early 1910s. The present day American Legion building on Greene Street was the union meeting hall for decades.

Today the mines are mostly gone, and their closing caused serious economic hardship for Silverton. The last operating mine, the famous Sunnyside, was closed in 1991, victim to unrelenting low mineral prices. The resulting lay-offs of 150 people caused San Juan County to have the highest unemployment rate of any county in the nation! In the foreseeable future there is little anticipation of mining resuming, so now Silverton has only historical links to the rough, daring occupation with which it is so closely associated.

At 9,300 feet above sea level, Silverton is one of the highest towns in the world. (Leadville, Colorado is even higher, but due to its location, has much less snow to contend with.) Winters remained a severe difficulty for miners even after the arrival of the railroad. Snowstorms, and the snow slides that followed, often blocked the train and critical supplies from Durango for months!

Locomotive #482 leads a train back to Durango. Before the railroad's arrival in Silverton, the journey to Durango was an arduous three or four days. Until 1968, the train out of Silverton had connecting service throughout North America.

Today, the train stops running in the late fall, and Silverton faces challenges in its efforts to remain economically viable through the winter months. But change is occurring; the Silverton Mountain ski area, opened in 2002, has already contributed a lot of life to winter business, and other outdoor pursuits seem poised to grow.

A touch of modern life has come to Silverton, with cell phone service and high-speed Internet. Another recent phenomenon is the boom in real estate prices, astounding to old-timers.

Silverton is a beautiful, peaceful place in winter, but the logistics of living here can still be difficult. The highways into Silverton are some of the most avalanche-prone in the country, and the rest of the world is locked out of Silverton (as town residents like to interpret the situation) with some regularity in winter. Even in the summer months Silverton lacks many of the amenities that most Americans take for granted.

It takes a special kind of person to appreciate life under such conditions. Silverton's residents are a unique group, and that is part of what makes the town special. Life has never been easy in Silverton but in many ways the town is still as tough as the rock its legacy was built upon.

Silverton is becoming a center for natural pursuits. This young lady looks at upper Cascade Creek from a footbridge on the Colorado Trail that links Denver and Durango.

The Christ of the Mines shrine was built under the direction of Father Joseph Halloran, with donations from people of all denominations. The shrine and the statue, carved from a 5-ton slab of Italian marble, were dedicated to the mining industry and the miners of the San Juans on August 24, 1959.

On Sunday June 4, 1978, the bottom of the high altitude Lake Emma gave way and flooded the Sunnyside Mine. The water flooded the underground mine shafts, but because it was Sunday, no miners were working! Many locals credited the miners' good fortune to this shrine.

This toll gate at Bear Creek Falls, between Ouray and Silverton, remained here from 1884 until 1900. The road that crossed the treacherous terrain took Otto Mears over eight years to build; price for a horse and rider was fifty cents, and a wagon was charged five dollars.

The D&SNGRR; photo by W. H. Jackson.

Otto Mears, Railroader

Otto Mears (1840-1931) is recognized as "Pathfinder of the San Juans" on a stained glass portrait located in the state capitol building in Denver, and he figured prominently in the development of southwest Colorado. Born in Russia, Mears was an orphan at age three, and immigrated to the United States when he was only nine years old. After he spent a couple of years in New York, relatives shuffled him to the bustling port of San Francisco, where he was supposed to meet another guardian. Young Otto never made the connection on the west

coast, and he was on his own from age twelve.

During his lifetime, the remarkable Mears showed capability in a variety of professions. He served as a soldier under Kit Carson in the Navajo campaign. He oversaw the construction of the Colorado capitol building in Denver, and it was his suggestion to plate the dome of that structure with brilliant gold leaf. He became a linguist with command of the Ute language and gained the respect of the Utes' Chief Ouray. Mears was interpreter and negotiator during discussions between Chief

According to legend, the Million Dollar Highway was named for the rich mineral content of the gravel used in grading the road. It follows the same route as the toll road built by Otto Mears that linked Ouray with Ironton and Silverton, through the steep Uncompahgre Canyon.

No railroad ever crossed this dramatic stretch along the route to Ouray, though Otto Mears had drawn up specific plans to do so.

Ouray and the U.S. Government that decided the fate of the rich mining land in the San Juans. Mears was instrumental in developing narrow wagon roads that served the mountainous mining areas of the San Juans, through some of the roughest terrain in Colorado. His first toll road, chartered by the Territory of Colorado, was built in 1867 over Poncha Pass to transport supplies, including Mears' own agricultural products, to the U.S. military in the San Luis valley. By 1884, his toll road network in southwest Colorado totaled 450 miles, much of which later became railroad lines. His most famous toll road, the breathtaking effort known today as the Million Dollar Highway, connected the mining camps of Ironton and Red

Mountain with Ouray. The northern portion of the road was blasted out of solid rock and was incredibly expensive in its day.

In 1887, Mears, always an entrepreneur, turned his focus from toll roads to railroads knowing that railroads offered him much greater profit potential. His first railroading venture was the Silverton Railroad. It followed some of the same course as his already established Ouray and Red Mountain Toll Road. The short line—narrow gauge, of course—ran 18 miles north from Silverton over spectacular terrain to the mining camps of Chattanooga, Red Mountain, and Ironton. The line terminated at Albany, at the north end of Ironton Park, where there was a loop for turning the train.

Silverton lies at the base of Anvil Mountain in the valley below, in this photograph taken near the top of Kendall Mountain, looking north.

Chatanooga Valley and the Mineral Creek drainage to the left was the route taken by Mears' Silverton Railroad, heading toward Sheridan (now known as Red Mountain) Pass.

The Silverton, Gladstone & Northerly ran along Cement Creek, right of Anvil Mountain.

The other line of Mears, the Silverton Northern, followed the Animas River toward its headwaters, just below to the right, going in a north-easterly direction.

Tracks from Durango enter down below, to the left, in this photo.

The Silverton RR line was completed to Red Mountain in the autumn of 1888, and on to Ironton the following year. The roadbed of the Silverton Railroad was nicknamed the "Rainbow Route" by Ouray newspaper editor David Day because of the arc it made ascending and descending Red Mountain Pass, known then as Sheridan Pass. The top of the pass, at 11,075 feet, made the Silverton RR the highest running line in the country. Operating a railroad at such an elevation was always a challenge. Unpredictable high-country weather plagued the Silverton RR, and operations were infrequent during winter.

Mears' line was an instant success. With the arrival of the railroad, mining operations in the Red Mountain district no longer had to rely on pack animals to get their ores to markets. Ore cars coming from Silverton were filled with coal and supplies for the miners. The Silverton RR profited from hauling passengers too, charging a hefty

This little gathering is celebrating the Silverton Railroad's first passenger train to the mining town of Red Mountain, September 19, 1888. The founder of the railroad, Otto Mears, stands next to the lady at the rear of the passenger car, while his chief engineer, C. W. Gibbs, stands near, third man from the right. The D&SNGRR

dollar per mile.

The Rainbow Route was an engineering feat with tight curves and steep grades. The chief engineer for the project, Charles W. Gibbs, knew the area well having already worked with Mears on his toll roads and, before that, as an assistant to the D&RG's Thomas Wigglesworth. The route taken by the Silverton RR had already been surveyed and considered by the D&RG in 1883. At that time, the D&RG elected not to complete the line for reasons not related to its potential profitability.

Connecting the Silverton line to the prosperous mining town of Ouray had been the ultimate aim of Mears. The last eight-mile stretch

from Ironton to Ouray posed a great obstacle even for the skilled engineer Gibbs; the design of conventional steam-powered locomotives simply could not cope with the extreme grade and hairpin curves. Plans were made to incorporate electrically powered locomotives to complete the eight-mile section between the two towns. In 1892, a specific survey was produced showing location and grade for the proposed Ouray-Ironton Electric Railway, including a complete spiral of rails down the steep cliffs surrounding Ouray. Mears felt he was so close to reaching his goal that he bought land in Ouray to use for a new depot.

Railroads in the San Juans were always influenced by the economics of mining, and the Silver Panic of 1893 forced Mears and his partners to abandon plans for the line to Ouray. Mining activity was severely curtailed throughout the Red Mountain district that was the heart of the Silverton RR. The railroad's schedule was cut, and the line was shortened, but the Silverton RR survived in some fashion until the ores of the area were depleted. The line was finally dismantled in 1926.

Another short line developed by Mears was the Silverton Northern that followed the Animas River toward its source, northeast of Silverton. A survey had been done from Silverton to Eureka in 1887, and two miles of track were built to a tramway of the Silver Lake Mill, as an extension of the Silverton Railroad, in 1892. Mears decided to form a second railroad not associated with the Silverton Railroad, which was then having problems with mining slowdowns after the Panic of 1893, and issues associated with rising water levels in the mines around Red Mountain. In 1895, the SNRR was incorporated as its own entity, and its directors expressed a goal of reaching the mining town of Lake City, over the formidable 12,640-foot Cinnamon Pass.

Lake City held obvious appeal then: it was more populous than Silverton or Ouray before the turn of the century and was also on a more direct route to Denver for the railroad. The immediate aim for the SNRR, however, was to lay track to the big Sunnyside Mine in Eureka ("I have found it" in Greek), adding a second large scale mine to their

line, and this was accomplished by the next year, 1896. The route followed a toll road that Mears had built to Eureka years before.

In 1903, the SNRR set out to construct a four-mile link to the Gold Prince Mill in Animas Forks, continuing along the same toll road, that would prove to be the most difficult of all of the lines that Mears would ever build. The steep, rough canyon along the Animas required significant digging and blasting. After numerous delays, the 400-man construction crew reached Animas Forks in November, 1904.

At Animas Forks the Silverton Northern installed a 50-foot turntable purchased secondhand from the D&RG, serving the same function as the one that had been used to turn trains at Corkscrew Gulch for the Silverton Railroad. The grade between Eureka and Animas Forks was incredibly steep—7% in spots. Locomotives of that era were able to pull no more than three cars up the line at a time; heading back toward Silverton, even when facing downhill, they led only four cars due to braking concerns.

The completed branch to Animas Forks provided financial relief to the railroad after the expensive construction effort that cost $27,000 per mile. The new mill at the Gold Prince mine was the largest in Colorado, capable of handling 500 tons of ore per day, and the SNRR got a huge influx of business.

Having reached Animas Forks, the SNRR was at the base of Cinnamon Pass, which led to the railroad's earlier stated objective, Lake City. However, several factors prevented any attempts at build-

The Silverton RR installed a turntable at this switchback on Corkscrew Gulch, near Red Mountain Pass. This was a very innovative concept in railroading, marking the first time a turntable, usually found in rail yards, was installed on a mainline. It was done out of safety concerns; when the locomotives were facing downhill, braking effectiveness was much greater. The turntable was used to reverse the direction of trains, one car at a time.

The Silverton Railroad quickly found it necessary to divert heavy snowfall with a cover over the turntable, pictured here, that was added one year after the railroad opened, in 1889. The D&SNGRR; W.H.Jackson photo.

ing over Cinnamon Pass: the grade would have been incredible, the weather on the pass often terrible, but most importantly, the economic motivation was just not powerful enough at the time.

The Silverton Northern offered luxurious passenger accommoda-tions for a short time. Mears acquired a Pullman car for the line that he named the Animas Forks. It was transformed into a combination sleeper and gourmet dining car that featured fresh oysters and an extensive wine list. Mears was always a smart businessman who recognized

This rare silver watch fob, attached to a classic Waltham watch, is now on display in the D&SNGRR Museum. Originally, it was good for free rides on the Silverton Railroad.

Mears treated his customers well. To celebrate the opening of each new railroad he built, Mears would distribute a series of passes that he had manufactured. Most were made of paper, but some passes were made of solid silver in a leather pouch. Those would go to select patrons and good friends of Mears. A few passes were even made of gold.

The passes made from precious metal are very sought after by rail afficiandos these days.

the benefit from the publicity the railroad would receive by offering such service.

During the winter the SNRR was constantly threatened with avalanches. Mears planned a series of wooden snowsheds to protect his line. Some of the structures were to have living quarters for snow removal crews who would be able to clear snow from the tracks on the spot. In 1906 a snowshed was built about a mile north of Eureka at the site of

one of the worst slides on the line. Mears' hopes for year-round operations were dashed when the structure was destroyed by a heavy slide soon after its completion. The upper portion of the line went back to a summer and fall schedule only.

The SNRR carried ores so rich that, for a time, armed guards rode along to protect the trains all the way from the mines above Silverton to the smelter in Durango.

The railroad continued to run until the Sunnyside Mine closed temporarily in 1939; by then track had already been torn up between Animas Forks and Eureka. The Silverton Northern wound up being the most successful of all of Mears' railroads out of Silverton because the mines along its route lasted the longest.

The third railroad out of Silverton associated with Mears was the 7 1/2-mile Silverton, Gladstone & Northerly. Gladstone was a sleepy town along Cement Creek that had been a mining and timber site since 1879.

The Gold King mine opened at the site of a promising vein discovered by a local miner named Olaf Nelson in 1887. Nelson did not really have the money to develop the mine, but he registered the claim anyway. He managed to dig a mineshaft and ship some profitable ore out of the Gold King before he died three years later, in 1890. After his death the mine was not worked for a few years.

In 1894, Nelson's widow sold the Gold King to a corporation that owned other mines in the area for only $15,000. Under new management the Gold King became profitable within a year. One shipment of gold out of Gladstone was valued at a record $180,000 per ton.

A large stamping mill was constructed adjacent to the mine. Steel stamping bars crushed silver and gold ore down to a size whereby the gold and silver could be separated from the rest of the rock.

It became obvious that a railroad was needed to the site, and Mears was originally approached about that prospect in 1898. At the time, Mears' Silverton Railroad was in receivership and he was not interested in another mining railroad. Gold King management and stockholders decided to build the railroad themselves, and the SG&N was constructed in 1899.

The new railroad helped the Gold King become one of the area's greatest producers, with total ore valued at over $8,000,000. Mining activity peaked in 1907. The mine was closed after a tragic fire in June, 1908 that killed six men. The Gold King eventually reopened but was closed again in 1910 due to labor and legal issues.

That same year Otto Mears and his son-in-law, James Pitcher Jr. decided to acquire the SG&N and take out a lease on the Gold King properties. The previous owners were happy to unload the declining line, and Mears was pleased to be able to consolidate the SG&N with his other lines into Silverton.

The SG&N had a sleeper car that once each week connected with D&RG trains to Alamosa and beyond. The benefit to the SG&N was mostly prestigious; it could advertise in its timetable that it had connecting service all the way to New York!

In 1911, catastrophic flooding washed out track on all of the Silverton lines, including the D&RG's. The SG&N, now called the Gladstone Branch, was almost totally wiped out. Repairs on the line took until 1913, when the Gladstone Branch began to run three trains a week. The line continued tenuously until 1938, when tracks were finally pulled up.

The three Silverton-based lines associated with Otto Mears crossed terrain that was previously thought impossible for railroad construction, with grades over 5% and 30-degree curves. Nor had anyone ever built railroads at such high elevations. The extreme high-country weather presented ongoing difficulties for all three lines. Despite these huge logistical obstacles, the Silverton-based railroads had few serious accidents and only one fatality in their history. To the great credit of Mears, they serve as fine examples of the creativity, ambition, and determination that fueled railroading efforts in the San Juans.

Animas Forks

Animas Forks was named for the west and north forks that converge here, forming the main channel of the Animas River. Early miners called the area Three Forks. Roads led from here to Silverton, Ouray, and Lake City.

Prospectors first wintered here in 1873, and just two years later, the town had its own post office. The community grew to 450 by 1885. A newspaper called the *Animas Forks Pioneer* was published for a time; the town's elevation of 11,200 feet made it the highest spot in the United States with its own paper.

There were more than five mines in the area, but few people stayed through the long, cold, isolated winters here. Most mining had diminished by 1891, but revived with the construction of the Gold Prince Mill in 1904. That same year, Mears' Silverton Northern Railroad arrived here, and this marked the terminus for that railroad.

The huge Gold Prince Mill processed 500 tons of ore each day, more than any mill in Colorado at the time. The ore was then loaded onto railcars, sent to Silverton, and on to the smelter in Durango. The Gold Prince Mill only lasted until 1910. Major parts of the mill were removed in 1917, to be used at another mill closer to Silverton, in Eureka.

William W. Duncan, a miner and mail carrier, built the distinctive *Bay Window House* , shown above in the foreground, in 1879, for himself and his family.

The last mining began to fade locally when metal prices fell worldwide, in the early 1920s, and Animas Forks soon turned into a ghost town.

William Henry Jackson's photo train is shown on the route of the RGS, stopped below Lizard Head Peak, heading toward Trout Lake, Rico, and Telluride.   The D&SNGRR; photo by W.H. Jackson

The Rio Grande Southern Railroad

In the hearts of railroaders, the greatest glory of Otto Mears lies in his creation of the Rio Grande Southern. The fabled 162-mile line went from Ridgway—nine miles north of Ouray—to Durango, linking Mancos, Dolores, and the mining communities of Rico, Ophir, and Telluride with the D&RG on both ends.

The circuitous route was another masterful piece of railroad engineering, crossing a spectacular and remote landscape. Mears' engineer was, as on his other lines out of Silverton, Charles Gibbs. Highlights of the line such as Lizard Head Pass, at 10,250 feet, and the Ophir Loop will forever be a part of railroad lore.

The Ophir Loop was a set of wooden trestles, some almost 100 feet high, with track curves that passed directly over rails underneath. It was built by workers that chiseled out the roadbed while dangling off cliffs more than 1,000 feet off the ground.

Mears hired a 3,000-man crew to construct the line, starting from both ends, in 1890. Help-wanted advertisements ran throughout the Rocky Mountains and attracted a diverse mix of Mexicans from New Mexico, Mormons from Utah, and European immigrants, mostly Italians and Irish.

The northern division worked on the section out of Ridgway. Their first objective was building over the Dallas Divide to Placerville, and then adding a 7.4-mile spur from Vance Junction to the rich mines in Pandora and Telluride. As with other railroads he had built, the right of way from the Dallas Divide to

Telluride followed a toll road Mears had put in place a decade earlier.

Mears was hoping to begin collecting some ore-hauling revenue to help pay for the rest of his big construction project. His hopes were realized; for a while Placerville was the second biggest freight-loading spot in Colorado, and Telluride mines loaded as many as 20 trains, each 10 cars long, in a single day.

Maintaining the sobriety of his work force was a serious problem for Mears. Purveyors of liquor set up shop a short distance from the work camp, and excessive drinking led to high employee absenteeism. Mears threatened to shut down his line to Telluride until San Miguel County quit issuing liquor licenses.

The southern division of the RGS started a line west out of Durango, their initial goal the nearby coal mines at Perins Peak. The spur to Perins Peak was quite a project in itself, with grades up to 4% and curves over 30 degrees. This section was designed and constructed by Thomas Wigglesworth, the engineer who had earlier surveyed the Durango-Silverton line for the D&RG. At its highest output, the Perins Mine filled three trains a day, supplying the RGS and the D&RG with 120 carloads of coal every week.

The town of Rico was so happy to have rail service that its residents had a big celebration before the line was connected on both ends. A number of dignitaries came into

town from the completed Durango side of the line. On October 15, 1891, the celebrants drove an inscribed spike made of silver, not gold, to honor the ore that was Rico's claim to fame.

The RGS officially opened for business in 1892, just two years after work had started, at a time when regional silver mines, such as those in Rico, were booming. Operations began quite successfully, with the RGS turning a strong profit its first year. But fate did not bless the railroad for long. The Silver Panic of 1893, and the subsequent plunge in silver prices, devastated the mining communities served by the RGS. Virtually overnight, hundreds of mines closed down, and it was said that most of the tickets that the RGS sold that year were one-way tickets out of the area.

The RGS was soon forced into receivership, and Mears lost control of the line. From 1893 on, the RGS operated as a separate entity, controlled by the D&RG. The RGS was not the only railroad hurt by the Panic of 1893; some of the nation's largest lines, including the Union Pacific and the Northern Pacific, also went into insolvency.

The RGS faced hardships almost its entire existence, seeming at times to exist by sheer determination and stubbornness. When mining revenues faded, the line was sustained by a huge timber industry that developed around stands of Ponderosa pine near Dolores and

Mancos. Millions of board feet of lumber were loaded onto RGS cars. After oil was discovered in 1924, near Bloomfield, New Mexico, the RGS was part of a link that brought thousands of Conoco Oil cars from Farmington to a Salt Lake City refinery. Starting in the late 1930s, some 1,500 cars of cattle, sheep, and angora goats were hauled to high summer pastures around Dolores, Lizard Head Pass, and Placerville. Some unique stock cars had two levels for livestock.

The area served by the RGS receives the most precipitation in Colorado. Before 1908 and the introduction of labor laws limiting the length of the workday, railroaders had to deal with being wet constantly because there was not enough time between shifts for their gear to dry out.

RGS crews faced daily challenges. They were almost always operating on a low budget, creatively using whatever means were at their disposal, like lots of bailing wire, to keep their equipment rolling. Track maintenance was less than thorough, and derailments were always a threat.

Writing about passenger travel on the RGS, author Mallory Hope Ferrell stated: "One person was born aboard the swaying cars, while a few others died—but most were only scared half to death." Other options for passengers were limited, since the RGS was the only link to the outside world for many of the

communities along its route. Most highways in this region were not upgraded until the 1950s.

Most of the locomotives operated by the RGS were aging and small 450s or 460s, of the K-27 class. Because those locomotives had a short wheelbase, compared to the 470s, they were prone to derailing on the poorly maintained RGS line. The locomotives would sway back and forth as they rode the uneven rails, and became affectionately known to railroaders as mud-hens.

In the 1940s, the RGS had the glory of hauling out much of the uranium ore that was used in the construction of the world's first atomic bomb, which brought an end to World War II. After more than six decades of service, the RGS ran its last train in the early 1950s.

A Galloping Goose is shown here cautiously crossing the lofty— 95' off the ground—wooden trestle well known to railroad historians as the Ophir Loop. Reportedly, on his first ride over the Loop, Otto Mears wanted to get off and walk.

The D&SNGRR

Galloping Geese visit the Durango-Silverton line during Railfest. In the foreground is a replica of Goose #1 built by Karl Schaeffer, and normally on display at the Ridgway Railroad Museum in Ridgway, Colorado.

The vehicles were originally called "motors" by the Rio Grande Southern, but they soon gained the nickname *Galloping Goose*, because their horn sounded like a honking goose, and they seemed to waddle down the poorly maintained, uneven tracks of the RGS.

The Galloping Goose

The Galloping Goose was a gasoline-powered vehicle adapted for the rails by the old Rio Grande Southern as a money-saving measure, starting in 1931. Its rather awkward look caught everyone's attention and became endearing to rail fans. With the nation in the throes of the Great Depression and with revenues for the railroad at historical lows, the RGS built the unusual motorcars to replace their scheduled train service on days when large capacity freight hauling was not needed.

Chief mechanic Jack Odenbaugh and superintendent Forest White designed the rail cars at the RGS' Ridgway shop. Other gasoline-powered vehicles, like the Casey Jones that operated around Silverton, had been running sporadically on the rails of southwest Colorado for years, and undoubtedly served as prototypes for the Goose.

Salvaged automobiles—Pierce-

Arrow Sedans and Buick-6s—were cut apart and spread to the width of a narrow gauge passenger car, then mounted on railroad wheels. The first Goose, Motor #1, as it was then called, only cost the RGS about $800 to build, and it paid for itself within the first month of its operation. The railroad estimated that a locomotive powered train cost .86 cents per mile while they could run the Goose for only .15 cents.

As they evolved, the Geese were equipped with some standard railroad equipment: air brakes, special headlights, and bells. The Pierce-Arrow six cylinder engines were quite powerful and capable of higher speeds than a normal train, though they averaged about 20 miles per hour, with fuel consumption around five and a half miles to the gallon.

The Geese carried passengers, some freight, and most importantly from a revenue standpoint, mail. After 1933, the Galloping Geese became the only scheduled runs on the RGS lines. Regular trains were added only when needed for hauling heavy loads of ore, livestock, or timber.

The move to the Goose saved the RGS $50,000 a year in expenses, mostly in labor costs. A Goose required only one motorman to operate, instead of a normal train's requirement of four or five crewmen.

Riding in a Goose was always an

In 1952, the Galloping Geese were used in the sad task of scrapping the Rio Grande Southern line, hauling away the same rails they had ridden. Goose #7 was used as a combination crane-flatcar in the process.

The Ridgway Railroad Museum

115

excellent adventure for passengers, and probably for the motorman as well. They were infamous for overheating, even when going downhill! Some of the old Pierce Arrows were outfitted with a temperature gauge in the radiator cap to signal the operator when to add more water from a roof-mounted water tank.

Their relative light weight, compared to trains, made them vulnerable to rocks, broken rails, and live-stock on the tracks. Breakdowns and minor mishaps, but no fatalities, became part of the lore of the Goose.

One inconvenience during a ride on the Goose was the lack of an onboard toilet. The RGS built little outhouses, some with Geese and Ganders painted on them, and placed them intermittently on the line.

Winters presented special prob-

The Casey Jones railbus was a predecessor of the Galloping Goose. RGS mechanics certainly studied it before they went to work building their own track vehicles from recycled automobiles in 1931.

The Casey Jones was built in 1915, with a gasoline-powered Maxwell engine (a Cadillac engine was installed during a rebuild in 1918), and a chain drive to the rear axle. Originally designed to be an ambulance servicing the Sunnyside Mine in Eureka, the modified Model T has room for 11 passengers. It was often used by mine officials to commute into Silverton.

In the photograph above, Jim Tofflemoyer is in a familiar position, tinkering with the Casey Jones, while Larry Beam offers encouragement. The Casey Jones is owned by the San Juan County Historical Society and alternates locations between Durango and Silverton. It sometimes rides the rails during special occasions like Railfest.

Some things just don't change: the Geese were always prone to mechanical delays. Wayne Brown, wearing the sun hat, and who did much of the work restoring this vehicle, Goose #5, finagles with the machine, along with 2 assistants.

lems: the Goose did not have enough traction to plow its way through much snow, so the RGS usually needed to clear the way by running a locomotive over the tracks after big storms. But that was by no means a guarantee the Goose wouldn't slip and slide on icy rails.

The RGS lost its profitable mail contracts to truck transportation in 1950. They tried to replace that substantial loss of revenue by increasing seating capacity on the remaining Galloping Geese, #3, #4, #5, and #7, which by that time were becoming very popular with rail fans. The boost in tourism sustained the railroad for another year or so, but the income generated was not enough to keep the RGS in business, and the

venerable line was scrapped in 1952. At the time not enough people realized that we were losing a national treasure.

You can still see and even take a ride on a Goose. The fully restored Goose #5, normally located at the rebuilt Dolores, Colorado Depot, is a regular attraction available to passengers at the D&SNG's annual Railfest. A fully operational Galloping Goose #1 was re-created by Karl Schaeffer in 2000, and is stationed at the Ridgway Railroad Museum. Goose #4, not currently operating, is on display at Telluride's San Miguel County Courthouse. The Colorado Railroad Museum in Golden has three Geese: #2, #6, and #7.

Mining in the San Juans

Miners found the San Juan Mountains a mineral treasure chest! The 12,000-square mile region contains some of the most mineralized country on the continent. The highest quality ores are concentrated into what is known as the San Juan depression, a caldera—the center of a long extinct volcano—that extends from Silverton to Lake City and is, on average, 15 miles wide.

The mountains surrounding the caldera—Kendall, Sultan, Grand Turk, and others—were at one time part of the volcano's cone. During intense volcanic activity, a host of

The Silver Lake Mine was located high above timber line in the Arrastra Basin, at 12,200 feet. Due to heavy snow, miners and a backlog of ore were unable to leave the complex for six months of the year.

The San Juan County Historical Society

This photograph shows the well-equipped machine shop at the Silver Lake Mine. The mine was operated by the enlightened Edward Stoiber, and working conditions were pleasant; the four-story boarding house had steam heat and good food. Drinking was prohibited because of its extreme effects at this altitude. The San Juan County Historical Society

valuable metals deep in the earth boiled up close to the surface. Subsequent glacial activity in the area gouged and scraped the rock on the surface, exposing the rich mineral veins underneath. Glaciers were active in the higher valleys of the San Juans as recently as 10,000 years ago.

The San Juans have hundreds of peaks over 13,000 feet and many over 14,000. The rugged, harsh terrain shaped the mining experience here.

Americans had their first experience with the thrill of "striking it rich" in the California gold rush of 1849. The gold found at Sutter's Mill in the Sierra Nevadas was plac-er gold; miners used the familiar technique of panning to separate gold dust or nuggets from other mineral deposits in streams and riverbeds. The gold found in California had originated in fissures in the granite formations there and had gradually been weathered away and carried into the drainages.

Most of the mining in the San Juans was of the hardrock variety. Most of the valuable minerals in the San Juans had to be dislodged from "lode" deposits. Lode describes a mineral vein encased in the rock where it was originally formed. To reach the vein, miners often had to dig tunnels or shafts into mountainsides and blast the rock surrounding

Arrastra Gulch, shown in the distance, high above, and just east of Silverton, was the site of the first organized mining operation in the San Juans, in the early 1870s. It remained a center of mining activity through the 1980s.

the vein into small pieces that they could then haul to the surface for processing.

Hardrock was an apt description of the mining style in the San Juans because the valuable mineral veins were lodged in extremely hard rock. To prepare the rock for blasting required drilling a pattern of holes. In "single-jacking," a lone miner would hold a four-pound single-jack hammer in one hand and repeatedly strike a cylindrical "drill steel," that he held and turned in his other hand. "Double-jacking" involved two men, one holding and turning the steel, the other swinging an eight-pound double-jack hammer.

Whether done as a team or individually, the work was agonizing and tedious, but it also required skill and precision. The holes were usually 30 inches deep; the steels had to be re-sharpened after going into only six inches of rock.

When the holes were deep enough, the blasting powder was set and then detonated with fuses of varying length, igniting the blasts in a sequence that would best break up the rock. After the explosion, the miners were left with a heap of rock, or "muck," which was loaded into ore carts. The process was repeated time and again, each blast clearing a volume of rock six to eight feet in diameter and to a varying depth.

Ore treatment was a primitive technology when mining began around Silverton in the early 1870s. Arrastras, from which Arrastra Gulch derived its name, were crude stone mortars where heavy stones were dragged around a circular pit of rocks, gradually grinding them into smaller pieces, revealing the gold. The arrastras were usually powered by burros or mules, and were sighted by early explorers in the San Juans, providing evidence of some Spanish prospecting in the region. In a resourceful advancement, output from the first mine in the San Juans, The Little Giant, was treated in a steam-driven mill.

If the ore was concentrated, the sorting was sometimes done by hand, especially in the early years when ore had to be transported to markets on pack animals. Stamp mills were the next evolution in rock crushing; steel stamping bars would break lump gold and silver ore into sand-sized particles to make it easier to separate from the rest of the rock and prepare the gold and

These miners are shown on an aerial tramway that served the Gold King Mine, located up the Cement Creek drainage, northeast of Silverton. There were other electrically-powered tramways in the area; they transported ore and workers from mines high in the mountains to mills and connecting railroad lines in the lower valleys.

The cables were supported on towers that might be 1,000 feet apart, allowing them to bypass difficult terrain. The towers were usually prefabricated and hauled up by mule teams.

Trams allowed miners to work year-round, giving economic stability to the entire region. The San Juan County Historical Society

silver for more processing. A smelter then continued the treatment, separating and extracting the different minerals by heating the ore to high temperatures. Smelters were tried on a small scale around Silverton, but they were not very efficient in the cool temperatures that are typical at higher elevations, and coal to fire them was not easily accessible. The railroad's arrival into Silverton and the new smelter in Durango fulfilled the needs of a large market in the San Juan mining country.

The D&RG developed a direct connection to the mining industry in Silverton. The Aspen Claim Group on Hazelton Mountain near Arrastra Gulch was organized in the 1870s, and remained one of the most consistently producing mines in the San Juans. The entire Aspen Mining Group was owned for many years by the D&RG and supplied the railroad with guaranteed ore shipments.

Mining spurred a great deal of technological innovation. Mechanization came to the biggest mines when cumbersome steam-powered equipment began to be utilized in the 1870s. Many of the mining towns in the San Juans, including Silverton and Telluride, were among the first in the nation to receive alternating current electric service, in the 1890s. Electrical power helped run equipment that dramatically increased mining productivity.

While mining is never an easy endeavor, in this remote region, miners faced an extreme climate, flooding, and avalanches. Inside, the mines were unpleasant places—cramped, dark, and either dusty or wet.

Because of frequent blasting in the mines, cave-ins and underground fires were always a threat. In 1901, an underground fire killed 24 miners at the Smuggler-Union Mine near Telluride.

Winters were sometimes brutal. Scores of miners died from exposure and pneumonia. Blizzards blocked the flow of food supplies for humans and livestock from lower elevations, even after the railroad arrived.

The steep, narrow drainages of the San Juans are among the worst areas in the world for snow slides. Avalanches not only knocked out the aerial tramways that took miners to and from work, the slides were a peril to the miners themselves. An avalanche destroyed a boarding house at the Shenandoah Mine near Silverton during the disastrous winter of 1906, resulting in 12 fatalities. Many more miners were killed in undocumented snow slides.

An old saying—"Mining can kill you a million different ways"—had basis in truth. Early mechanical drills were called widow-makers because they created clouds of pulverized rock dust that miners absorbed into their lungs with deadly consequences. Later "wet" drills helped to lessen the dust, but the underground environment was still filled with peril for miners. Poor ventilation in the dusty, smokey mine shafts caused dangerous levels of carbon monoxide, especially in the smaller, independently-owned operations.

Water seeping into mine shafts created another huge problem for miners, especially those in the Red Mountain mining district that included the towns of Ironton and Red Mountain. The water would combine with iron sulfides, creating very corrosive sulphuric acid. The acid ate through miners' clothing and anything made of metal in the mines–nails, cables, and tools–creating dangerous working conditions. The constant battle with sulphuric

The scale of mining efforts in the San Juans is evident in the 1903 photograph, below, of the Silver Lake Mill, located just north of Silverton. The line serving this mill belonged to Otto Mears' Silverton Northern Railroad. Locomotive 281, leased temporarily from the D&RG, is shown moving cars. The mill was demolished for salvage and burned in the late 1940s. As you can see in the photograph above, only the foundation of the Silver Lake Mill remains today.   The Center for Southwest Studies, Ft. Lewis College.

The Red Mountain Building is an old boarding house in the Red Mountain mining district.

acid was a major factor leading to the closing of mines in this area.

Prosperity spread throughout the mining country of the San Juans in 1890, when the United States Congress passed the Sherman Silver Purchase Act. After almost 20 years competing with bankers from the eastern states, who wanted to keep gold prices high, western silver-producing states—advocates of "free silver"—finally saw success. The Silver Purchase Act directed the U.S. Mint to purchase 54 million ounces of silver each year and to coin silver dollars.

Silver prices soared to over one dollar an ounce, and fortunes were made in the San Juans. It is estimated that Silverton had more than 100 working mines at this time. Worldwide economic factors, however, continued to put pressure on gold and silver prices. Banks began to hoard gold, depleting the U. S. Treasury's supply and leading to the Panic of 1893. Boom days of local mining ended abruptly when the U.S. government, after months of filibuster by Western senators, decided to repeal the Sherman Silver Purchase Act on October 30, 1893.

The action precipitated a worldwide economic slump, and locally, the effects were devastating as silver prices plummeted. Many mines closed immediately, and miners fled the area, soon followed by the bankers and merchants who were supported by them. Some mining towns in the San Juans that relied on silver, like Rico, never recovered from the economic downturn. Other towns, like Silverton and Telluride, were ultimately able to survive because their ores had sufficient gold content.

The issue of union representation within the mining industry was marked by a bitter and violent struggle that began in the 1890s. By that time, mining had become big business and individual miners could not compete with the large companies to obtain mining claims. Wealthy industrialists, like Guggenheim, purchased large holdings in the San Juans, and many mining operations had become, basically, company towns. Many miners felt like they had become little more than laborers working $3-a-day, 7 days a week, with faint hope of achieving the dreams that had gotten them involved with mining in the first place. They found themselves toiling long hours in an, often unsafe environment. The miners decided they needed to assert themselves with the mines' owners to achieve any changes.

Management, predictably, felt threatened by the workers' demands for better pay and working conditions, and sought the government's protection from strikes. The miners were led by the Western Federation of Miners, whose leaders were self-proclaimed socialists. The situation became polarized and volatile. Meanwhile, the sympathies of the public were mixed, many fearing the bloodshed that had come to be

This group of workers, most likely coal miners or operators of coke ovens, stands near a coal chute that feeds waiting D&RGW gondolas, probably at the base of Smelter Mountain in Durango. Coal was taken by rail up to Silverton where it fueled many heating stoves. Coal was also converted into coke, in ovens at the base of the mountain. Coke burned hotter than untreated coal and was used to fire the Durango smelter.

The La Plata County Historical Society

This is the Old Hundred boarding house, built on Galena Mountain, adjacent to the #7 level mine, around 12,250 feet above sea level. The Old Hundred Mine was named after the Bible's 100th Psalm. The mine never made enough to pay off the investment that was made to get it operational. This structure has been stabilized since this photo was taken. Silverton lies off in the distance to the northwest.

associated with unionization.

Telluride was a flashpoint in the labor struggle. In 1901, miners there went on strike demanding a $3, 8-hour workday. One union miner was killed in a confrontation with scab workers at the Bullion Tunnel of the Smuggler-Union mine. Despite the fatality, striking union members pre-vailed in that episode and scabs, some beaten, were marched over Imogene Pass and told to stay away.

The general manager of the profitable Smuggler-Union, Arthur Collins, who was trying to break the union, was killed by a shotgun blast through the window of his home on November 19, 1902. Murder charges were brought against local union members, but the evidence was weak and there were never any convictions in the case.

Miners went on strike again in 1903, this time in sympathy with miners in Cripple Creek. Governor Peabody of Colorado, fearing a recurrence of the earlier violence and in alliance with local mine owners, sent units of the Colorado National Guard to physically remove the striking miners from the area. They arrived in Telluride aboard an RGS train armed with a Gatling gun—an early version of the machine gun—mounted on a coal car in front of the locomotive. The strikers were locked in "bull pens" on Telluride's main street and then loaded onto RGS rail cars and shipped to Ridgway, or even as far away as New Mexico and Kansas, where they were ordered to never return. One group of strikers was dumped out at the top of snowy Dallas Divide in the middle of winter.

The campaign against the Western Federation of Miners continued over the next year and a half, with union members facing threats and harassment from thugs who had been hired by the mine owners. The strikers had to admit defeat, but bitterness remained for many years.

Both sides in the struggle were guilty of abuses. The Colorado militia, in coalition with the mine owners, blatantly disregarded the constitutional rights of the union miners, while union leaders did not discourage the use of bombings and violence to achieve their aims.

Near the end of 1904, management at the Smuggler-Union mine agreed to the one of the strikers' principal objectives, $3 for an eight-hour day, and other mines followed suit, but management refused to hire anyone who had ever been a union member.

In Silverton, organized labor was

This shaft house sits upon a vein of silver that went straight down about 1,200 feet at the old Yankee Girl mine in the now deserted town of Red Mountain.

From 1882 until 1898, the vein yielded ore worth $100 million in today's dollars.

The structure is in a state of disrepair, but new owners plan to stabilize and preserve it.

The Mountain Top mine and boarding house in Governor's Basin is located high above Yankee Boy Basin, near Ouray, Colorado.

firmly entrenched in mining and mills from the early 1900s until the onset of World War II. Silverton avoided most of the violence that characterized the labor movement in southwest Colorado, and became a community that was, in many ways, held together by union membership. Durango also had unions but they were never as powerful as Silverton's.

Mining in the San Juans was initially for gold, and silver followed, but what kept the mining industry going until World War II were the less exotic base metals—lead, copper and zinc. Gold and silver became profitable by-products for mining operations.

After World War II, the area experienced a great decline in mining activity, and the 1950s were hard years for Silverton. Due to low freight activity, the D&RGW ceased year-round service in 1952, and operated only during the summer when tourism was highest.

The last large-scale mining near Silverton ended with the closure of the legendary Sunnyside Mine and the Mayflower Mill in the summer of 1991 because of low metal prices, especially for zinc and lead. While the potential still exists for re-opening mining operations in the area, at this time it seems doubtful.

Mining has always been a source of dreams fulfilled, and unimaginable wealth, and conversely, hardships and bitter disappointments. As the object of such passion, mining has provided a rich legacy for the San Juans and the railroads with which it was so essentially linked.

Stony Pass, the road visible on the right side of this photo, led to the mining camp of Howardsville, in the valley far below. The summit of the pass was over 12,500 feet above sea level.

Stony Pass

Stony Pass was the favored way into Silverton before the arrival of the railroad in 1882. The road led from Del Norte, then one of Colorado's larger banking and commercial centers that had once been in consideration for the state capitol.

The route followed the gentle grade of the Rio Grande River until changing dramatically as it reached the Continental Divide, at 12,500 feet. The descent into the San Juan mining communities was steep and treacherous.

Sure-footed pack animals were the preferred method of transportation over Stony Pass; wagons had to be disassembled and roped down over rough stretches. The route was reportedly littered with broken wagon parts and discarded supplies, testimony to the difficulty teamsters faced.

Still, a lot of freight crossed into the booming mining camps. In 1872, the equipment to start Silverton's first sawmill, weighing more than 6,000 pounds, was brought in by a team of oxen. Luxury items like pianos, fine china, and hand-carved wooden bars were to follow.

In the winter, ambitious travelers would trek over Stony Pass on foot at night, their way illuminated by moonlight. The evening's colder temperatures would solidify the snowy crust to keep them from breaking through.

Denver & Rio Grande surveyors considered a route to Silverton through Del Norte and over the Continental Divide at Cunningham Pass, not far from Stony Pass. It would have been the most direct path from Denver, but the prospect of maintaining year-round access at such an elevation dissuaded them.

The Engine Crew

Monty Caudle, engineer, in a photograph taken from a flatcar being pushed by the locomotive.

Locomotive engineers achieved the status of American folk heroes when the risk-taking Casey Jones became a legend in the early 20th century. It is easy to understand the fascination with train engineers: for decades, when American life revolved around trains, they operated the fastest vehicles in the world.

Today's engineers for the D&SNG do not try to set speed records, but they continue the engineer's most important function—safely operating the locomotive. Driving the powerful and sophisticated machines at their command requires years of experience along

with a focused presence of mind. As an engineer for the D&SNG, he will be expected to calmly accept the risk and responsibility inherent in the job.

After checking over the locomotive in the morning to be sure it is in top working order, the engineer spends his workday in constant vigilance, continuously shifting his gaze from the tracks lying before him to inside the cab—the steam pressure gauge, the water glasses, the air pressure gauges of the braking systems—and back again.

An engineer normally spends years as a fireman before being promoted to the right side of the cab. He gains so much familiarity with the mechanics of the locomotive that most problems will be noticed long before they become an issue.

The second half of the engine crew is the hard-working fireman. He will shovel approximately five tons of coal from the tender into the firebox on a round trip to Silverton! But his duties are not all brawn; he must also respond to the locomotive's ever-changing power demands. With experience, the fireman memorizes changes in grade along the entire route and can anticipate the locomotive's need for increased or reduced power.

Each locomotive has unique tendencies in steaming. Increased power, of course, requires more coal, but adding more coal than needed can be counter-productive. Especially in the K-28s (470 series

The fireman, Steve Otten, places each 20-pound "shot" of coal with accuracy, to maintain an even firebed.

locomotives), fires are prone to "getting slugged" when coal is piled too heavily on top, smothering the flames underneath.

The fireman regulates the amount of water coming into the boiler and the heat of the fire to keep the steam pressure that is needed. While doing this, he must also keep a watchful eye on the steam pressure gauge and the water glasses to ensure safe and efficient operation of the engine.

Ever observant, the fireman is the engineer's assistant, taking signals from the train crew, ringing the bell, and watching the tracks, especially on left-hand curves. In their spare moments, firemen observe the engineer and become very familiar with

the operating procedures of the locomotive.

Most firemen aspire to become engineers, but they often work for years honing their skills and reading operating manuals in their off time. To qualify for a position as engineer, the fireman must complete a series of three progressively more difficult tests.

The D&SNG often places accredited, practicing engineers in the cab to perform as firemen. In fact, many employees of the railroad swap positions to learn more about different aspects of the operation and to get in a few extra hours of work during slow times of the year.

Turning the hand brake wheel, as shown left, spins a shaft that pulls the brake-shoes together against the wheels, stopping the car.

Brakemen for the D&SNG still use these manually applied brakes to "tie down" a car whenever needed, using a "brake club" to turn the wheel with leverage.

Today, air-brakes are activated by compressed air that the engineer controls from inside the locomotive's cab.

Norm Rathmell, with his right hand on the butterfly fire door lever, points to the boiler pressure gauge; to get optimum power from the boiler, the fireman learns to coordinate the flow of cool water from the tender with the heat in the firebox. Norm has retired from the D&SNG.

The Train Crew

Rich Millard, chief conductor, signals to the engineer while approaching a flag stop.

The conductor functions on your train like the captain of a ship. Historically, he is the person responsible for the safe operation of the train, management of the crew, and the comfort and safety of passengers. All of the train crew operate under the conductor's supervision; train orders are given jointly to the conductor and engineer, but the conductor has ultimate authority to direct the action, signaling train stops and starts.

Conductors are called upon whenever decisions have to be made concerning train operations. Your conductor has reached a high level of railroading expertise and is thoroughly familiar with the operating rules and practices of the D&SNG. In the event of a delay, the conductor will contact the dispatcher to see if adjustments in the schedule are necessary. He also makes certain that his train displays the proper flags or lights.

The conductor's knowledge of mechanics is extensive, especially pertaining to the portion of the train that stretches behind the locomotive—brakes, couplers, windows, heating systems—the conductor is familiar with it all.

The conductor tries to blend his technical and procedural knowledge with people skills—assisting passengers, solving problems with reservations, and, of course, answering questions.

The other half of the train crew is the brakeman. Brakemen have a good general knowledge of the train's braking system and help perform the brake tests that take place before and during every run. A "standing air" test is done before the train leaves Durango or Silverton, and a "running air" test occurs just after the train starts moving. The brakeman checks the air pressure gauge at the rear of the train and communicates to the conductor or engineer the status of the system.

A large part of the brakeman's responsibilities involve train logistics; helping to switch cars, lacing up brake lines, lining (probably short for aligning) switches, all the

133

Brakemen use hand signals to communicate with the engine crew. Bob Kuhn, on the left, with two hands up, is signaling that the locomotive is within a distance of 1/4 car or less to a stop.

The brakeman on the right is about to give the engineer a "stop" signal as the locomotive slowly backs up to couple with the boxcar.

Coupling requires coordination and a deft touch. The locomotive's speed must be just right to allow the coupler's knuckles to close without excessive force.

You've probably heard the phrase "It was so quiet you could hear a pin drop." The expression comes from joining couplers together so quietly you could hear the pin go "clink."

Currently, almost all switching in the Durango Yard is done with diesel locomotives to minimize the amount of soot released in town.

while communicating by hand signals to the engineer. While not the experts that conductors are, brakemen are familiar with all of the mechanical operations of the rail cars, and they make periodic inspections of the wheels and brakes on all of the coaches to ensure that everything is functioning properly.

While they're on the train, brakemen spend much of their time watching for any mechanical problems and helping to maintain a safe environment. They often lend the conductor a hand collecting tickets and, of course, answering questions.

In their earliest configurations, trains were stopped with brakes on the locomotive, but as trains grew longer and heavier, brakes were added to the railcars. The initial braking designs required the brakeman to tighten down an iron wheel on the tops of the railcars with a wooden club. The brakeman would scamper precariously from one car to the next, setting and releasing brakes as needed, in all kinds of weather. Obviously, the job was very difficult and dangerous, and many brakemen lost their lives in the process, from exposure to the elements, losing their footing, or in collisions with low-hanging tunnels. The brakeman's ominous position atop of the cars was called "decorating."

A refined automatic air braking

system designed by George Westinghouse around the early 1870s was a vast improvement. The system, basically still in place today, would activate automatically if line pressure was interrupted. Most railroads in that era resisted the installation of air brakes due to their cost until required to by government regulations. The Westinghouse air braking system has proved its worth ever since, greatly reducing the dangers to the hard-working brakeman.

Whenever the train stops, an important duty of the rear brakeman is to guard the rear for oncoming traffic. Ron Keiser, shown here signaling to the engine crew, carries with him an arsenal of warning devices—red flags, percussion charges called torpedoes, and flare-like fusees—that he can deploy as needed.

After the running brake test has been completed successfully, one of the train crew, the brakeman or the conductor, will give the engineer the highball or high wave of the hand; the engineer will acknowledge with two short whistles, and your train continues on its way.

Concessions

Working uniforms have changed over the years, but concessionaires remain essential to an enjoyable ride on the D&SNG.

The concessionaires are an important public face for the railroad throughout the day's ride. Besides keeping passengers nourished and happy, they are a valuable source of information. The concessionaires have a close working camaraderie with the train crew.

The D&SNG has four concession cars, all with long histories. Concession Car 212 dates from 1879, when it was a 45-passenger coach named Caliente—hot in Spanish. It is the oldest car still in regular use by the D&SNG. Concession Car 126 was originally a baggage car built by the D&RG in 1883. Concession-Baggage Car 64 dates to 1889, when it was constructed as a mail-baggage combination car. Concession Car 566 was built as a mail car in 1888. It was converted into an excursion car, before the D&SNG remodeled the coach for concessions.

Sarah Jaksha, Mary Stoffel, and J. Leigh Mestas
Photo by Yvonne Lashmett

Each familiar with the task at hand, Maintenance of Way crews have a fluid, almost choreographed, approach to their projects. This crew is shown replacing old railroad ties. Mechanization has eased much of the drudgery—the machine in front pulls out the firmly embedded old ties—but the work is still demanding.

Each 55-pound tie has a life of about 30 years. The goal is to replace about 3,500 ties each year—a big expense for the D&SNG.

Maintenance of Way

Maintenance of Way (way is short for the railroad's right of way) keeps the D&SNG's 14-man crew busy. Their unflagging efforts are responsible for keeping the 45-mile line—track, switches, bridges, road crossings—in good repair so that trains can operate safely.

Most of the crew seem to enjoy being railroaders, spending a lot of time outdoors, even though the work is often rough. Former MOW crewman Ron Rivera summed up the attitude this way: "You really

have to like working to be out here."

For several of the MOW crewmen, railroading is in their blood—they are second or third generation employees of the railroad.

Many of the tasks they perform take years of experience to master, and some of their skills with sledge-hammers, or spiking mauls, are rapidly becoming lost arts. While MOW crews still use a full cart of manual tools, the D&SNG owns a million dollars worth of maintenance equipment: two "Speed-

Tangled rails north of Tacoma, after the flood of 1970, provide a dramatic demonstration of the river's power.

Within a few short weeks after the devastation pictured above, Maintenance of Way crews for the D&RGW had rebuilt the roadbed and completed most of the track repair.

The temporary wide spread of the railroad ties allowed track-cars to transport workers and materials farther up the line before everything was put back in place.   The Allan C. Lewis Collection

Demetrio Martinez worked on Maintenance of Way for both the D&RGW and the D&SNG, from 1957 to 2001.

Swings," capable of traveling on the tracks or on the ground, are multipurpose machines. With attachments, the Speed-Swing can perform as a backhoe, snowplow, frontend loader, or boom. Other specialized equipment used by the MOW crew includes tie machines, ballast regulators, tampers, and spiking machines.

Rail is replaced as necessary. Depending on the location of the rail (whether it's on a curved or tangent track), the amount of traffic it receives, and how well the track bed is maintained, rail can easily last 50 to 70 years. Most of the rail on the Durango-Silverton line was rolled in the old Pueblo, Colorado steel mill between 1898 and 1913, and was relayed here after it was used elsewhere on D&RG sytem.

Rail is typically broken by rock, mud or snow slides. Whenever a patrolman spots a bad length of rail, he checks the rail's length, and the "punch pattern" (the distance of the drilled bolt holes from the end of the rail, that must match the existing angle bars that hold two rails together), and relays that information to the railroad dispatcher. The dispatcher informs MOW, and a crew is dispatched to replace it, usually with the help of a Speed-Swing to load ties and rails onto a push car.

The train's off-season is a time of increased activity for MOW. The right of way of the railroad extends about 50 feet on both sides of the track, and crews perform wildfire maintenance during the winter and early spring. Brush is cut back, controlled fires burn overgrown groundcover, and trees that are growing too close to the tracks are removed.

Leon Montoya, chief welder for the D&SNG, has worked for the railroad since 1988.

Track Patrolmen

Walker Taylor

Track patrolmen for the D&SNG, spending their days driving back and forth through some of the finest scenery on earth, are thought by some to have the best jobs on the railroad. But there is a serious side to their duties; as the eyes and the ears of the railroad, they are a solitary guard working out in front of the train and once they discover a problem, the tranquility of their environment can change quickly.

Patrolmen are their own bosses and are fully responsible for resolving any problem that they encounter. Sometimes they can make the repair with their own resourcefulness; they carry the wrenches, hammers, and pry-bars to make many basic repairs to the rails. Other times they may be required to radio for assistance, and then give the dispatcher in the Durango yard an accurate description of the problem at hand and its precise location.

In the winter and spring, as temperatures fluctuate between freezing and thawing, causing movement of the earth, the patrolmen run ahead of the train looking for fallen rocks and other hazards on the tracks. Summers are the toughest for the patrolmen: when conditions are dry, fires can ignite from the locomotive's sparks and cinders. The patrolmen following the train have to be constantly vigilant, trying to quickly extinguish any spot fire with the water tank they carry along on their cars. Since the fires of 2002, patrol cars with a three or four-man crew pulling a 300-gallon water wagon and 400-foot hose follows all trains. The crews are trained by the D&SNG, following U.S. Forest Service wildland firefighting technique.

The motorized cars are sometimes called *speeders*, and they are the fastest vehicles on rails between

John Martinez retired in 2005 after 42 years of railroading on the Silverton Branch. He usually drove the early morning advance patrol car up to Silverton and had an incredible knowledge of the line. John stayed in great physical condition and was legendary for doing pushups on the rails.

Durango and Silverton, capable of speeds over 30 mph.

The railroad recently added to their fleet of patrol cars. The new vehicles, built by Les King Motorcars, are recognizable by their lighter yellow color—the older Fairmonts are painted Rio Grande Gold. There are some major upgrades; the new cars have four-cycle motors with electric starters, instead of the noisy two-cycle engines and hand-crank starters on the older Fairmonts. The new machines require less fidgeting than the temperamental older cars as well; the only drawback to the new

cars is their weight that makes them harder to set off the tracks.

The dispatcher in Durango regulates patrol cars, like every vehicle on the rails. Drivers must radio in to receive a "block" of time over a given section of track and keep a written record of their communications.

Patrolmen are taken from the ranks of MOW workers, and they know every foot of the line between Durango and Silverton. Anything out of the ordinary is usually noticed and dealt with before it becomes a problem.

The most physical part of the day for track patrolmen can be getting their cars back on the track. Mac McCoy, third generation railroad employee, demonstrates the proper technique: once the wheels of the 550 pound machines are in contact with the steel rails, they pivot pretty easily.

Early on, the D&RG found that it was often more expensive to maintain their lines than it had been to install them. Ballast needed to be placed around the ties to make the track more stable.

These center-dump gondolas, or "hopper" cars, that locomotive 478 is pulling out of Silverton were obtained in 1982 from the East Broadtop Railroad in Mount Union, Pennsylvania, to haul ballast for the D&SNGRR. It is estimated that they have been used to carry over 200,000 yards of gravel from rock-crushing plants in the Animas Valley to upgrade the line between Durango and Silverton.

The Animas River

While human history began along the river more than 2,000 years ago, the Spanish explorers Escalante and Dominguez gave it the name Rio de las Animas Perditas, meaning River of Lost Souls, on August 8, 1776. Their visit to southwest Colorado occurred about 80 years before the first Anglo-Europeans arrived. The exact reason for the ominous-sounding name is not known. Perhaps the Spanish learned early on how treacherous this river could become.

The Animas River accompanies the D&SNG along most of its 45-mile line, and the river has provided the railroad with benefits and challenges. The continuing success of the railroad can be attributed, in part, to the spectacular scenery along its route. The Animas is not only a part of this landscape, its erosive power has created much of the spectacular geology between Durango and Silverton.

On the other hand, the river has periodically dealt railroad operations on the Silverton Branch some severe disruptions. There have been three 100-year floods (that occur, on average, every 100 years) in the history of the railroad here, in 1911, 1927, and 1970.

The 1911 flood was the worst, developing after a huge storm dumped four inches of rain on Silverton. Normally, water flows in the Animas peak at around 5,000 cubic feet per second; in October 1911, flows reached a raging 25,000 cfs! The railroad bridge in Durango was partially destroyed, and 22 miles of track in the Animas Canyon above Rockwood were ripped loose and deposited randomly along the river's banks in twisted heaps. The remains of washed-out rails are still visible along the riverbed, enduring testimony to the river's power. Railroad operations on the Silverton Branch ceased for 63 days after the 1911 flood, while repairs were made under the supervision of Otto Mears.

The Silverton Branch was saved from demolition in 1970 when the D&RGW decided to replace the six miles of track that had been washed away in floodwaters that year.

Surprisingly, the worst floods in this region have occurred in the fall, not during the spring runoff. In the spring, cooler nights in the high country tend to moderate the pace of the snowmelt, and the natural drainage system can usually accommodate the runoff. In the autumn, low-pressure systems sometimes stall over the San Juans and rain can persist for days. Soil cover in the San Juans is thin, and the ground becomes saturated after a relatively

After the flood of 1911, the D&RGW knew the river's potential for destruction. Flooding recurred in 1927, when this dramatic photo was taken, and the railroad again placed loaded gondolas on the trestle in Durango, hoping the extra weight would keep the bridge supports from being washed away. This time the bridge held, although looking at the sagging rails, repairs were needed.

small amount of rainfall. When the soil cannot absorb any more precipitation, all of the rain that follows becomes excess, and drainages overflow.

When the water is high, the river is almost unrecognizable. The volume of water entering the Animas, combined with the river's relatively narrow, straight bed creates a force so great that boulders the size of houses can be swept along the river's path.

The leaching of mine tailings into its tributaries has historically caused water quality in the Animas to suffer, but that was never the only source of contamination. Not unlike rivers around the world, the Animas once served as an all-purpose trash dump and sewer system, even when the river was the source of Durango's drinking water, around the early 1900s. Local citizens were understandably upset back then, and it was decided to make the Florida River the primary source for clean city water. A nine-mile pipeline was built to carry the water to the reservoir that is still in use today.

Water quality in the Animas, once very discolored even in Durango, began to improve in the mid-1930s when the town began to use landfills to dispose of trash, and rudimentary sewage treatment became operational. About the same time, a new state law required mine tailings to be deposited on land instead of into rivers. Heavy mineral deposits would still leach into the waterways, but the problem was greatly reduced. Efforts to clean up the mining byproducts continue today. Tailings are being removed and placed in "glory holes" that contain the leaching. Another part of the current strategy is to divert the drainage from the old mines so contaminated water does not enter the Animas. These ongoing pursuits, along with natural filtering, point toward a healthier future for the Animas.

The river is proving to be quite

Today the Animas River is prized for its recreational benefits. When the river is up, Durango residents are apt to hop into their kayaks during lunch breaks.

resilient. Water from the Animas is now part of Durango's water system. A stretch of the Animas running by Smelter Mountain and the sewage treatment facility has been designated "Gold Medal" waters by the Colorado Wildlife Commission, considered to provide the highest quality fishing in the state for large trout.

Locomotion: the power to move

"The locomotive is more than a machine, it is almost a living being...it breathes..." Michel Chevalier, French economist, 1839.

Few, if any, man-made creations capture our imaginations and stimulate our senses like steam-powered locomotives. On a cool Durango morning, when the doors of the roundhouse swing open, and the hissing, clanging, churning iron horse ventures forth to meet the day, you know you are in the presence of a rare and special mechanical invention.

The steam locomotive transformed this country, creating the most mobile nation on earth. Before the railroad's introduction into the West, this country's population was highly concentrated along the east coast, and most people did not venture far from home. Steam power

changed all that, and travel in America became second nature.

Trains and the steam locomotive have made a cultural imprint on our national psyches, reflected in our music, our language, even in the pace of our lives. Railroad timetables gave Americans an orientation to scheduling that never existed before.

The steam-propelled locomotives in the service of the D&SNG were built during the 1920s. By that time, steam technology had evolved considerably from its rudimentary beginnings. Steam power was an integral part of the Industrial Revolution that began in the 18th century.

Engineer Steve Otten, his left hand on the straight air brake valve, performs the standing air brake test before leaving Cascade Canyon Wye. The throttle is diagonally above his left hand.

Although their design is sophisticated in many ways, these locomotives were designed before much was known about ergonomics; the engineer spends his day constantly moving his grip from the throttle to the brake valve, which can get tiring.

In 1769, the Scottish inventor James Watt patented his design of a steam-powered engine that converted steam power into a more efficient rotary, rather than reciprocating (back and forth) motion. Cornish engineer Richard Trevithick produced a working model of the steam-powered locomotive in 1797, and in 1804, he successfully tested a locomotive that pulled five cars, ten tons of iron, and 70 passengers.

The potential of steam-power was obvious from earliest designs that showed a high pressure steam engine capable of moving five or six times its weight. The boilers in those early steam engines could tol-erate only 50 pounds of pressure per square inch; advances in design allow the powerful locomotives belonging to the D&SNG to operate efficiently at 195 to 200 psi!

Early locomotive designs in this country were modified from European models to meet specific American needs. Powerful locomotives were specifically designed for the vast, open spaces of the West, emphasizing load-hauling capacity over speed. When narrow gauge lines were constructed, engines were specifically designed for use on the lighter rails. The narrow gauge locomotives were generally smaller, lighter, and built with a shorter wheelbase to handle sharp curves.

The locomotives used today by the D&SNG are among the last, heaviest, and most refined narrow gauge locomotives ever built. They are of two types or classes, K-28s and K-36s—designations that are based on the wheel and driver arrangement, and the pulling power of the locomotive.

The K represents the nickname for a Japanese locomotive design known as Mikado. The Mikado design configuration was "2-8-2," as denoted by a system created by Fredrick Whyte around 1900 where the wheels of a locomotive are designated by their location. So, the 2-8-2 locomotive has two non-powered, pivoting wheels (pony trucks) in front, eight driving wheels connected to driving rods that are powered by the engine's pistons, and two non-powered trailer wheels (trailing trucks), under the cab of the locomotive. The pivoting wheels in front guide the locomotive through curves, minimizing the potential for derailing, while the trailing wheels help maintain the locomotive's stability through curves when pulling heavy loads. Earlier locomotive designs, known as Consolidations, did not have the trailing wheels.

The number 28 or 36 describes the locomotive's pulling, or tractive power, in thousands of pounds. Thus, the tractive power of the K-28s with tenders is rated at 27,500 pounds, and K-36s are capable of pulling 36,200 pounds. Both classes

of locomotives are astoundingly heavy: the K-28s with full tenders weigh 254,500 pounds, while fully loaded K-36s weigh 286,600 pounds. That helps explain why you can feel the earth move as they pass by.

The 470 series of locomotives, K-28s, were ten engines designed for passenger service by the D&RG and manufactured for them by the American Locomotive Company in Schenectady, New York, in 1923. Of the original ten that were built, only three 470s remain, and they are all owned by the D&SNG.

The United States Army requisitioned the seven others in 1942. The U.S. feared a Japanese invasion of North America via the Bering Strait. To counter such a possibility, the U.S. planned to build a narrow gauge line into that remote area of Alaska to transport troops and supplies. The line was never built and the seven 470s were shipped back to Seattle. Unfortunately, the seven locomotives were dismantled for scrap in 1946, just years before their historic significance would have been recognized.

Locomotives 473, 476, and 478 operated on many parts of the D&RGW's system prior to the 1950s. 473 served frequently on the legendary "Chili Line" that operated between Antonito, Colorado and Santa Fe, New Mexico until that line was abandoned in 1941. Locomotives 478 and 476 saw extensive service on the San Juan

According to Steve Jackson, Vice President of Mechanical Operations, "When a steam engine has a problem, mechanics need only about 10 minutes to diagnose it and about 10 hours to fix it. For the diesels, the times are reversed."

passenger train that operated daily between Durango and Alamosa until 1951. For many years, the San Juan was the most important transportation link that residents of southwest Colorado had to the rest of the world.

From the 1950s through 1980, the trio of 470s were the only locomotives operating on the Silverton Branch and are well known to many rail-fans and locals. Today the 470s are used mostly on double-headers, when extra power is needed to pull long trains up to Silverton, and on trains with nine cars or less.

The D&RGW had the 480 series of locomotives built in 1925 by the Baldwin Locomotive Works in Philadelphia, Pennsylvania. Known as K-36s, the ten engines were the last narrow gauge locomotives to be constructed in this country. They are considered by railroaders to be the

most powerful design of narrow gauge locomotives ever made, especially efficient in pulling heavy loads.

Occasionally one of the 480s ran through Durango and up to Rockwood during the D&RGW years, but never as far as Silverton because bridges on that section of the line were not constructed to handle these heavier locomotives. The 480s were used in freight hauling on other parts of the D&RGW's narrow gauge network, and they sometimes pulled the San Juan passenger train between Durango and Alamosa.

When the Silverton Branch was purchased from the D&RGW, the deal included two K-36s and four K-37s (490 series), along with the three familiar K-28s. Today the D&SNG owns four K-36s: 480, 481, 482, and 486. Five others—483, 484, 487, 488, and 489—

150

belong to the Cumbres & Toltec Scenic Railroad. In an unfortunate accident, locomotive 485 fell into the turntable pit at the Salida yard in 1955 and was scrapped for parts by the D&RGW.

Locomotive 481 had been completely overhauled by the D&RGW during the 1960s. It was stored in the Alamosa roundhouse until 1967, when it was towed over the tracks (without being fired-up) to Durango. Here it remained outside in the Durango Yard for years. When the locomotive was inspected by the D&SNG in 1981, everything was still in pretty good shape. The roundhouse crew completed a few necessary repairs to the boiler, and after extensive structural upgrades were made to the Durango-Silverton line above Rockwood, locomotive 481 became the first of the K-36s to see service to Silverton in August, 1981. Today the K-36s are the workhorses for the D&SNG, pulling most trains out of Durango.

Rusted-out locomotive 480, also part of the deal with the D&RGW, was moved to Durango from Alamosa by truck and trailer over Wolf Creek Pass in 1981. After years of expensive restoration work in the Durango roundhouse, it was placed back into service in 1985.

The D&SNG obtained locomotive 482 in an exchange with the Cumbres & Toltec Scenic Railroad for locomotive 497. The line of the C&TSRR between Chama, New Mexico and Antonito, Colorado

does not have the sharp curves of the Silverton line, and the larger 490 series of locomotives serves them well.

Locomotive 486 had been on display at the Royal Gorge suspension bridge near Colorado Springs until 1999, when the D&SNG was able to negotiate an exchange for another of its 490s, locomotive 499.

Locomotive 486 needed a major overhaul in the Durango shops. It is estimated that the D&SNG invested $250,000 and over 10,000 man-hours in the restoration project. Locomotive 486 made its first run on August 26, 2000, during the Railfest celebration.

Builder's Plates for the American Locomotive Company, ALCO, are bolted to the side of the boiler jacket on the D&SNG's 470s.

ALCO was the nation's 2nd largest locomotive manufacter, building more than 75,000 steam locomotives. In consortium with General Electric, they later made many diesel locomotives.

Locomotive Basics

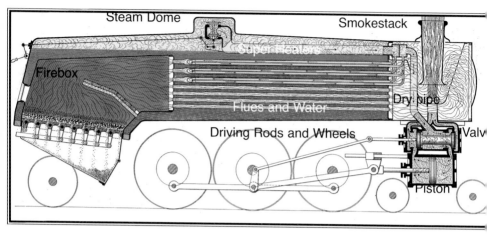

The basic operation of a steam-powered locomotive requires heating water—lots of water—until it becomes steam.

The tender, located behind the locomotive, carries the coal and water used to create steam-power. The fireman shovels coal from the tender through the firebox door. The air in the firebox, shown in red, becomes very hot and is drawn into the flue pipes, which run through the boiler. The hot flues are surrounded by water, colored blue, and heat the water until steam, colored yellow, is produced.

The steam rises to the highest point on the locomotive boiler, the steam dome. When the engineer opens the throttle inside the cab, a throttle valve (the valve controls the amount of steam that passes through) inside the steam dome delivers steam via the dry pipe into the system of yellow flue pipes known as superheaters. In the superheater units, the steam is exposed to firebox heat again and becomes even hotter, and thus more powerful.

The superheated-steam is directed through the steam pipes in the smoke box to four cylinders, two on either side of the locomotive, located just in front of the driving wheels. The upper cylinders contain valves and the lower cylinders contain pistons. The pistons are driven back and forth by the valve-controlled steam pressure, pushing the rods that turn the driving-wheels of the locomotive. The driving wheels set the locomotive in motion.

Steam exhausts into the smoke box and out the smokestack, along with combustion gasses and smoke from the firebox.

The D&SNG's current 65-foot turntable was installed in 1924 to accommodate the larger locomotives of that era, replacing the original 50-footer. The turntable is powered by an air compressor that is inside the roundhouse. This turntable is one of the few still operating in the world.

Below, heavy, semi-circular shaped counterweights, seen here near the bottom of their cycle, ride outside the driving wheels. The counterweights balance the weight of the drive rods and help to maintain the momentum of the driving wheels. The plethora of steam shown here is coming from the opened cylinder cocks that expel water from the cylinders.

Diesels

Currently, the D&SNG uses their diesels to move cars in the Durango Yard, and to power special trains.

During the 1960s, the D&RGW worked diesel locomotive #50 (now at the Colorado Railroad Museum) in the Durango Yard. Decades later in 2002, the D&SNG purchased their first diesel to pull trains whenever the fire danger grows too high. The roundhouse crew did an expedited remodel on the vintage 50-ton locomotive, and it was operational within two weeks. The Diesel #1 was named Hotshot, affirming its fire-fighting role.

The D&SNG wound up buying four more diesels in 2002, all of them in a state of disrepair. It was reported that more than 1,100 hours went into rebuilding locomotive #7. In March 2006, the D&SNG purchased two 90-ton diesels.

Diesel locomotives became popular for several reasons, but primarily due to their huge advantage in maintenance costs, compared to labor-intensive steam locomotives.

Though not as powerful as steam locomotives, diesels were more fuel-efficient. Water stops were no longer needed—a huge savings in time and infrastructure. Supplying parts was much simpler because diesel locomotives were much more standardized than steam-powered.

General Electric manufactured the first commercial diesel locomotive in 1918. Designs improved, and in 1924, G.E. joined ALCO, the American Locomotive Company, to produce and market the engines that would soon dominate the railroading industry. All of the diesels owned by the D&SNG were made by G.E., weighing between 50 and 100 tons.

Diesel locomotives should perhaps be called diesel-electric locomotives. A diesel fuel-burning engine turns a generator that produces electricity. Electric power is what turns the axles of the locomotive.

The Roundhouse

The D&SNG Roundhouse currently has nine working bays to service the labor-intensive locomotives. During peak season, the emphasis is on keeping the engines operational, and the roundhouse remains a busy place after sundown. At the end of their daily run to Silverton, engineers will report to mechanics any issues that need attention, and the roundhouse crew works hard to remedy any problem by the next morning.

Fires in the locomotives are kept alive after their daily service. It takes many hours for the boilers to reach steaming temperatures, and if this process were to be rushed in the morning, damage could occur to the boiler's steel. The night crew will let the steam pressure in the boilers drop from 190 pounds to about 150 pounds. The night watchmen will begin to rebuild the pressure in the boilers at about 5 a.m.

Before they are moved out of the

Upon returning to Durango, most locomotives are pulled into bay 9, on the left. Inspection pits around the bay enable the crew to get a good, close look at things. After servicing, the engine is repositioned to make room for the next locomotive.

While in service during the busy summer season, the boilers are drained and cleaned out once a month. Most locomotives are moved inside the roundhouse for major overhauls during the off-season.

The D&SNG operates a world-class machine shop. These locomotive driving wheels have been turned on a huge lathe here to eliminate any worn or flat spots.

Locomotive's steel wheels, or tires, are applied by heat-shrinking them onto the driver wheels, using a device called "the ring of fire."

New wheels on passenger cars and tenders are bored a very slight diameter less than their axles, and are pressed on under at least 100 tons of pressure.

roundhouse and onto the turntable, the locomotives are carefully checked over, fittings tightened, and greased. An Alemite pneumatically powered grease gun is used to lubricate fittings on the engine rods and bearings, where main rods and side rods are connected to the locomotives' driving wheels. These guns, and the zerk fittings they insert grease into, were designed in the 1930s and saved hours in labor time. All of this lubricating is designed to keep friction that can quickly destroy locomotive parts to a minimum.

Major overhauls are done on the locomotives during the winter, when the roundhouse is a cacophony of banging, drilling, hammering, and grinding. Every 15 years, a steam engine's boiler must be disassembled, serviced, and inspected. The Federal Railroad Administration oversees the major boiler repairs.

The types of skills needed to work on the old locomotives are unique, and in today's world there is not much training available to workers outside of the hands-on experience they gain working here. New hires usually have a strong mechanical background or experience in electrical work.

With the attached machine shop, the roundhouse is a completely self-sufficient operation; most parts are fabricated within the facility. What the machinists don't make, they buy at the local hardware store.

Danny Webb, Boilermaker

The machine shop is one of the largest steam locomotive repair facilities in the United States. It houses massive machine lathes and drill presses that date from the 1940s—the last machines that were ever manufactured specifically for working on steam engines. Many of these tools had been sitting idle for decades in warehouses around the world before they were acquired by the D&SNG, following the round-house fire in 1989. One of the last known quartering machines—needed to make critical repairs on loco-motives—was purchased from the South African Railway.

On an environmental note, the D&SNG, working together with the City of Durango and the State of Colorado, added $300,000 smoke scrubbers to the roof of the round-house in 2001, substantially lessen-ing the locomotives' exhaust to the outside. The sophisticated system uses water to capture particulates in the coal smoke and convert the gas to liquid.

Other steps have been taken: locomotives are kept under the scrubbers as long as possible to minimize the amount of coal smoke emitted outside. Roundhouse crew-men start up locomotive fires using cleaner burning oak logs instead of coal, and fireboxes are watched closely overnight to make sure fires are burning cleanly and efficiently.

Gary Clark, Engine watchman

Marshall Chavez works on one of the new diesels that have been com-pletely refurbished by the D&SNG.

Danny Webb is in the cab of one of the steam locomotives. Look at the size of those wrenches!

A new sand house and sand tower have been constucted recently to replace the original facility, built in the 1880s.

The level in the sand dome, the forward dome on top of the loco-motive, is checked and topped off daily. Engineers control the release of sand to the top of the rail, underneath the drivers, to gain greater traction when rails are wet and slippery.

During the summer season, evenings are a busy time in the Durango Yard. The firebox is cleaned out by shaking the ash grates underneath the fire from inside the locomotive's cab.

The hot ashes drop into the ash pan, and when the ash pan is opened, the ashes fall into the ash pit, pictured below. This procedure keeps the fire burning cleanly through the night. In the morning, the firebox receives a more extensive cleaning before the locomotive heads out on its daily run.

Roundhouse workers get dirty and greasy while doing their jobs; the D&SNG provides a laundry service for their clothes.

Roundhouse Fire!

Locomotives 473 and 476 are shown here beneath a heap of charred timbers following the roundhouse fire. The D&SNGRR

The blaze ignited sometime after midnight on February 10, 1989 in the roundhouse that was originally built in 1882. The exact cause of the fire was never conclusively determined.

Oxygen and acetylene tanks exploded and added fuel to the blaze; temperatures inside the roundhouse were estimated to have reached 2,500 degrees! All six of the operable locomotives then belonging to the D&SNG were in the building. Locomotive 473 was closest to the machine shop, and caught the full brunt of the heat. 473 had just been overhauled and was ready for operation, its tender full of coal.

Unfortunately, the coal added more fuel to the fire.

For a while that night it seemed the blaze was almost under control, but when firemen had to reset their positions, the fire caught a second wind. The roof of the roundhouse collapsed on top of the locomotives, inflicting considerable damage. At that point, firefighters gave up on controlling the blaze and kept their hoses aimed on the engines, trying to keep them cool.

The restoration process began immediately, and debris was cleared within a week. Thankfully, all the locomotives were salvageable, though some required considerable repair. The roundhouse crew set up shop outside and worked with purpose and determination. Their enthusiastic efforts were aided by mild spring weather that year, and not one D&SNG timetable run was missed.

The roundhouse fire brought a lot of publicity to the railroad; news of the event made the front page of the *New York Times*. Rail-fans from all over the world offered their help and contributions.

The original roundhouse had been built with ten stalls, constructed of red brick with a wooden roof. A new 36,000-square foot round-

house, with 17 bays (nine used for locomotive servicing and eight used by the D&SNGRR Museum), was dedicated exactly one year after the fire, February 10, 1990. Its architecture complements the original design and even incorporates the southwest wall that survived the fire.

Obviously the fire was destructive, but it resulted in some unexpected benefits: the new roundhouse is larger and has improved access for working on the locomotives. It also features one of the finest railroading machine shops in the world.

This aerial view of the roundhouse shows the full extent of the devastation incurred in the blaze.   The D&SNGRR

The Car Shop and the Rolling Stock

The D&SNG operates a 4,000-square-foot car shop that was completed in 1982, and is staffed by a year-round crew of twelve versatile carmen, some of them primarily carpenters. The facility houses separate woodworking and welding shops, along with a professional painting booth, to maintain the D&SNG fleet of 46 passenger cars.

During the off-season, the car shop is as busy as the roundhouse. Every car is brought into the car shop, trucks removed (trucks are the entire frame underneath the railcar at either end to which the springs and four wheels are mounted) and wheels pulled off for inspection and maintenance, along with a thorough check of the rest of the car. The car shop crew takes care of any problems that arise, from brakes and leaf springs to plumbing and heating systems.

The D&SNG coaches are a mixture of fairly modern rolling stock and some of the oldest cars remaining from the early days of the D&RG. Carmen study original plans to duplicate any missing parts on the coaches, and they are masters at matching old materials. Today many cars have interchangeable parts and the same safety features.

The cars have two braking systems, automatic and straight air. If air pressure is lost due to a broken line, or for any other reason, the automatic braking system will

Car shop foreman Ray Ludwig.

engage and stop the train. Both braking systems are operated from the locomotive cab.

Brakes are activated by air pressure that causes brake shoes to contract against the coaches' metal wheels, thus stopping the train. Hoses connect the brakes to a steam-driven air pump (that makes the thumping sound) on the locomotive, delivering the air pressure. The air brake hoses are visible around the couplers between each car.

The D&SNG operates 24 closed coaches, all of which are virtually indistinguishable from one another. Twelve of the closed passenger cars were built by the D&RG between 1879 and 1889. These cars have seen numerous modifications over the years.

In 1923, all passenger coaches of the D&RGW had their wheel size changed from 30 to 26-inch diameter to lower their height off the

The original Silver Vista, shown on page 15, was a popular glass-topped observation car built by the D&RGW in 1947 that was destroyed by a fire in Alamosa in 1953. A new Silver Vista was unveiled by the D&SNG for the opening of the 2006 season.

Its frame was built by Melcher Brothers Iron Works of Durango, with the rest of the work completed in the D&SNG car shop. A blend of the old and the new, the Silver Vista features low-e safety plate glass, offering some protection from the southwest Colorado sun, and reconditioned Hale and Kilburn walkover seats. These seats will enable passengers to take in the view facing either direction.

ground and give passengers easier access. For winter use, forced-air propane heaters have replaced coal stoves. Other cosmetic changes have made the coach interiors more durable and easy to clean.

Increased tourist traffic on the Silverton Branch prompted the D&RGW to manufacture eight passenger coaches in 1963 and 1964, the first new narrow gauge cars they had built since 1904. While they closely resemble the older coaches, they were the first cars of metal construction. Window frames were aluminum and the siding was steel,

beveled to replicate wooden tongue and groove.

There are 17 open observation cars or gondolas in use today. They have bench-like seats running lengthwise, so passengers can enjoy the scenery without having to turn their heads. They are #400-416; most have been built from recycled components that originated on old standard gauge boxcars or stockcars.

Of the group, #400-405 have an interesting history. In 1953, the D&RGW needed more cars to serve booming freight traffic to natural gas fields along the Farmington

163

Carman Jim Martinez started working for the railroad in 1971. Carmen inspect under every coach twice daily, looking for any problems with brakes and wheels. Brake shoes sometimes need to be replaced after only 30 days in service. Repairs are made quickly since during the peak summer season every passenger car is needed.

Branch. They cut down some standard gauge boxcars, creating specially designed narrow gauge cars with open ends and reinforced sides, to haul pipe and culverts for drilling operations. In 1963, after the traffic to Farmington slowed, the D&RGW reworked six of these pipe cars into the open gondolas #400-405 for passengers on the Silverton Branch. The other open observation cars, #406-416, were built in-house at the D&SNG car shop, between 1982 and 1986.

The D&SNG operates some of the oldest passenger cars in existence— #257, #270, #291, and #311. These cars were built for the D&RG in 1882, by the famous carmakers Jackson & Sharp, who began manufacturing railroad cars in 1865. These cars featured Buntin

walkover seats that could be adjusted to face in either direction.

The Alamosa parlor car is another product of Jackson & Sharp in the D&SNG fleet, built in 1880, as a Horton Chair Car. These rather upscale cars had individual reclining chairs (think wooden Lazy-boys), instead of the bench seats that were used in coaches for lesser fares. The Alamosa was originally known by the Spanish name Hidalgo, reflecting the aspirations of William Jackson Palmer to reach Mexico City. The car was later used on the elegant daily passenger service between Durango and Alamosa, known as the San Juan, during which time it was re-named Alamosa. While it served on the San Juan, the Alamosa was equipped with kitchen and buffet facilities, steam heat, and comfortable accommodations for just 14 passengers.

The San Juan ceased operating in 1951, and in 1957, the Alamosa—then the last parlor car on the narrow gauge lines—was stripped of its kitchen and became a passenger coach on the Silverton Branch. In 1981, the D&SNG again rebuilt the Alamosa for use as a parlor car. Today it is used regularly and features a bar, tables, and chairs for 24 passengers. Four other passenger cars in use today for the D&SNG—#312, #313, #319, and #327—were also in service on the San Juan.

The D&SNG car shop has faithfully restored three private cars, the Cinco Animas, the General Palmer, and the Nomad, to their splendid original condition. These cars are painted Tuscan Red, the color first used by the D&RG on their special business cars.

The D&RG built the private car now known as Cinco Animas in 1883, for use as an immigrant sleeper. In those days, immigrant sleepers were designed with few amenities, to transport impoverished newcomers to this country for low fares. Emphasis was placed on high seating capacity, giving little consideration to passenger comfort. The original car had seats for thirty passengers, with Spartan bare plank bunks overhead.

This car has experienced numerous remodels and restorations in its long history; it was turned into a business car for the D&RG in 1913.

In 1963, five individuals known as the Cinco Animas Corporation purchased the car and gave it its present name. In 1982, the Cinco Animas was sold to the D&SNG and today it can be chartered for private use.

The General Palmer, built in 1880, also served as a business car for the D&RG. In later years, the D&RGW allowed it to fall into a state of disrepair. A former passenger remarked that snow would blow in one side of the car and out the other. It has been beautifully restored by the D&SNG at a cost of $250,000, complete with mahogany siding and original brass fixtures, along with modern amenities such as satellite Internet service. It was brought back into service during Railfest 2001. The General Palmer is used exclusively by the D&SNG's current owner, Allen Harper, his family, and guests.

The private car Nomad is discussed on the next page.

The four historic concession cars are discussed under the section on Concessions, page 136.

Combination car 213, named Home Ranch, has a specially designed hydraulic lift to enable boarding for wheelchair-bound passengers. The car was built by the D&SNG in 1983.

The ornate Victorian private car Nomad retains much of its original beauty. Luxurious touches include red velvet sofas and draperies, a bedroom with a brass bed, marble-top dressers, a private bath, and a kitchen.

The private car Nomad was built as an economy class chair car by Billmeyer and Small of Pennsylvania in 1878. Originally named the Fairplay, it was rebuilt as Business Car N in 1886, and became part of a small, well-appointed Executive Office Train that included dining, sleeping, and observation cars. Reportedly, this car was the favorite of William J. Palmer, president of the D&RG.

The Fairplay was involved in a train accident in January 1917, known as the "Millionaire Special," described under milepost 468.2 on page 55.

The Fairplay has hosted numerous dignitaries, including U.S. presidents William Howard Taft, Ulysses Grant, Theodore Roosevelt, and Gerald Ford. The car was renamed Nomad while it was owned by several private parties between 1951 and 1982, when it was acquired by the D&SNG. It is now the oldest private railroad coach still in service in this country and is available for private charter.

Close Call

At approximately seven in the morning on June 25, 1987, the driver of a commercial truck overloaded with 20 tons of potatoes lost control of his vehicle coming down Highway 160, about 10 miles west of Durango. The highway has wide, sweeping curves, but the grade is a steep 6% in places. The driver tried to slow his speed by scraping the side of the truck against the highway's guardrail, but to no avail. At the bottom of the hill, he went through a green light at the intersection of Highways 160 and 550 going an estimated 110 mph.

Upon reaching the angled embankment at the edge of the Durango Yard, the truck became airborne! It ripped through the perimeter chain-link fence, and moments later collided into the side of locomotive 473 that was sitting just beyond the coal dock, ready for its morning run to Silverton.

The exact location of the crash was fortuitous; had the locomotive not been positioned exactly where it was, the truck would have continued through the yard, into a waiting trainload of passengers. 473 needed more than $50,000 in repairs, but due to the structural strength of the 127-ton engine, and because impact was not directly on the boiler, a massive explosion was narrowly avoided.

Just before impact, the truck driver lowered himself onto the floorboard, and, incredibly, suffered only a broken leg and ankle. His was the only injury that occurred in the accident. Two roundhouse mechanics tending to the locomotive, John Hood and Gilbert Sanchez, had just enough warning to get out of harm's way. It took over an hour to cut open the crumpled cab and release the very vocal driver.

A few fortuitous Durango residents helped themselves to the huge bounty of spuds that was scattered around the yard that day.

Reportedly, the truck driver never got behind the wheel of a commercial vehicle again—he became a preacher.

The truck's trailer was split open, and 40,000 pounds of potatoes were scattered all over the coal loading dock in Durango. Well known Amos Cordova, Vice President of Traffic and Public Relations at the time, is shown walking away from the mess.
The D&SNGRR

167

The Caboose

The celebrated and universally recognized caboose was designed to provide shelter for the train crew, and a vantage point of the train from the rear, especially on freight runs when no other car provides an unobstructed view. The watchtower-like cupola on top dates back to the American Civil War.

From the caboose, the conductor and brakeman helped coordinate the train's movements with signals to the engine crew. On modern trains, most cabooses have been replaced by more high-tech equipment, but many railroaders feel that nothing can replace the eyes and ears of actual trainmen riding behind the line of cars.

The word "caboose" came from a similar sounding nautical term, meaning a wooden cabin on a ship's deck where cooking was done. Railroaders of old sometimes called the caboose a "crummy," as in a "crummy place to live." There were many other nicknames, none really complimentary. The humble caboose was never elegant, prone to being too hot or too cold, and not especially clean.

Cabooses #0540 and #0505 are shown just above Elk Park where they are being utilized by snow-clearing crews in early spring.

Three conductors for the D&RGW are caught at a relaxed moment on board caboose #0540 in this photo dated 1954. From left are Alva Lyons, Myron Henry, and R. S. Murray. Note that the caboose is equipped with a coal-fired cook stove and sleeping bunk.

In the early days of tourism on the Silverton Branch, passengers were served coffee that conductors had brewed up in the caboose, providing a lot of goodwill for the railroad. The D&SNGRR.

There are three original D&RG wooden cabooses still in service for the D&SNG, all built in the 1880s. The larger cabooses, #0505 and #0540, have a 25-foot body and a total length of 30 feet. MOW and crews on work trains use both of these cabooses frequently. Caboose #0505 is stocked with provisions to provide shelter and food for railroaders. Caboose #0540 is a mini-warehouse, carrying the most commonly needed tools and supplies.

Caboose #0500, a diminutive 17 feet long, was built in 1886 and was originally known as D&RG Caboose #1. It was sold in 1950 to Bob Richardson, the well-known railroad photographer, and founder of the Colorado Railroad Museum in Golden. Richardson had it on display at his Narrow Gauge Motel in Alamosa. In 1987, #0500 was purchased by a business in Cripple Creek, where it was again put on display. The D&SNG acquired the caboose in 1993 and has beautifully restored it to original condition. Caboose #0500 is available for private charters.

The Red Apple Line

The Denver & Rio Grande constructed a 45-mile extension from Durango south to Farmington (known earlier as Farming Town), New Mexico in 1905, to give the railroad access to the rich coalfields in the San Juan Basin. The D&RG anticipated strong demand for the coal from mainline railroads out of Gallup, New Mexico, so they built the Farmington Branch with standard gauge rails to facilitate potential connections. The demand never materialized, and no other lines ever connected with Farmington.

For years, the Farmington Branch, the last line of the San Juan Extension, was used primarily to haul agricultural products from orchards around Aztec and Farmington and became known as the Red Apple Line. For a while, a daily passenger train operated between Durango and Farmington.

The Durango Yard was built to dual gauge, with three rails on wider ties, to accommodate both narrow and standard gauge equipment. Still, it was difficult for the D&RG to transfer freight from its narrow gauge rails in Durango to

the standard gauge after it had already done so in Alamosa. It was also problematic for the Durango Yard to store the equipment necessary to maintain the two gauges of track.

In 1923, the D&RGW gave up its hope of connecting the Farmington Branch to other lines, and the broad gauge rails were converted to narrow gauge—perhaps the only instance this ever occurred! The actual task of converting the 45-mile line to narrow gauge was reportedly accomplished in just one weekend, with three hard-working crews pulling up one rail of the track and scooting it over on the ties.

In 1924, oil was discovered in Bloomfield, New Mexico and Conoco oil tank-cars that had been converted from standard gauge were loaded in Farmington and hauled to Durango. From Durango, some of the oil was sent west to a refinery in Salt Lake City, and some east to Alamosa and beyond.

In the 1950s, Durango and the Farmington Branch were given a boost by the discovery of large oil and gas reserves underneath the coal deposits of the San Juan Basin. The most practical way to haul in the miles of pipe and other needed drilling supplies was on the D&RG's old narrow gauge line. The D&RGW, however, was seeking to abandon its line between Alamosa and Durango at that time and found itself in the awkward position of not

Moving pipe bound for the San Juan Basin in New Mexico from standard to narrow gauge cars took place in the D&RGW's big yard in Alamosa, Colorado, shown here.
Transferring freight between the different gauge lines was always a problem for the railroad.
The Aztec, New Mexico Museum

wanting the extra business. (A similar predicament would face the railroad years later when it wanted to drop service on the profitable Silverton Branch.) The D&RGW actually tried to persuade the El Paso Natural Gas Company to use truck transportation instead, and El Paso actually had to use legal means to compel the D&RGW to move the freight!

Throughout the 1950s and into the 1960s, trainload after trainload of pipe manufactured at the CF&I steel plant in Pueblo, Colorado, a facility originally founded by the D&RG, went west to Farmington.

The 490 series of locomotives (K-37s), the largest engines on the narrow gauge lines, were frequently used to haul the heavy loads. The 490s had originally been built for use on standard gauge rail in 1902, but were converted to narrow gauge by the D&RG in the late 1920s.

Demand for drilling supplies in the San Juan Basin began to diminish in the early 1960s. The Red Apple Line survived a few more years, primarily by hauling livestock.

The Farmington Depot was reduced to splinters by a huge natural gas explosion in 1964, and replaced for a while by a steel building. The end of the Farmington Branch, the westernmost reach of the D&RGW's narrow gauge operations, came when track was dismantled in 1968. Stretches of the old roadbed out of Durango can be seen above the east bank of the Animas River, and an old water tank is visible closer to the state line.

Winter Woes, Winter Wonder

In this unusual perspective, a crew of shovelers is shown trying to clear a snowslide off a buried D&RG locomotive in the Animas Canyon not far from Silverton in 1920. The Allan C. Lewis Collection, Photo by Frank Duca

Winter is a time of special beauty in southwest Colorado, but operating a railroad at this time of the year requires a lot of extra effort. For much of its history here, the D&RG ran to Silverton year round, and had to deal with snow and snow slides that made other obstacles like steep grades, sharp curves, and high altitude, pale in comparison. Snow was an awesome logistical challenge, and this was at a time when disruption of the railroad's schedule was not merely an inconvenience; around Silverton, thousands of people and their livestock depended on the railroad to supply their basic needs.

There are 13 verified slides along the upper Animas Canyon, between Needleton and Silverton. Closures due to avalanches occurred almost every winter, lasting anywhere from hours to months. The rotary snow-plows designed by Thomas Wigglesworth that served the railroad well on Cumbres Pass could not be used here because the snow slides in the canyon contained rocks and branches that damaged the blades of the rotary plows. The crews working for the D&RG had to dislodge the snow and debris one shovelful at a time.

Snow slide removal is not like clearing snow off of your sidewalk;

SACUACHE SNOWSLIDE, 60 FEET DEEP.
ANIMAS CANON D&RG NEAR SILVERTON, COLO.
BRUMFIELD, BERT, PHOTO.OURAY

The 60 foot-deep passageway shown here was cleared one shovelful at a time. Saguache Snowslide refers to the spot we call Snowshed Slide today, MP 492.5. This photo was taken sometime before the snowshed was constructed in 1890 by the D&RG. The San Juan County Historical Society.

avalanche material takes on the consistency of cement—very heavy and compacted. Sometimes it was removed in igloo-like blocks.

Snow slides weren't the only problem; high winds causing blowing, drifting snow periodically frustrated snow removal efforts by filling in areas that had already been cleared.

Crews of two to three hundred men—often miners unable to get to work—were employed as shovelers. For their exhausting efforts in the cold, they received about $1.50 a day. Gravesites at the Silverton Hillside Cemetery prove that some of these men died in the struggle to

173

This 1920 photograph shows a D&RG locomotive pushing a huge snow plow, trying to clear the roadbed in the Animas Canyon near Silverton. By that time, the engines had become powerful enough to move much of the heavy snow out of the way. The Colorado Railroad Museum;

keep the rail line open.

During the winter of 1883-84, the train to snowbound Silverton was blocked for 73 days. Lives hung in the balance, and hardy snowshoed residents of Silverton hauled supplies all the way from Needleton, 14 miles away. In the winter of 1890-91 even Durango was snowed in! Rockwood reported a snow pack four feet deep, and this time the railroad was blocked from Silverton for 53 days.

The worst winter on record was probably in 1905-06. During the early months of the winter, the D&RG had trouble even getting trains from Alamosa to Durango, due to deep, drifting snow on 10,000-foot Cumbres Pass. The worst storms on the Silverton Branch that season waited until March.

On March 17, 1906 the Silverton Standard reported that the D&RG line was "packed in like solid ice." Spring snows in the San Juans often have a high moisture content that easily compresses. Snow was piled so high in the Animas Canyon that workers had nowhere to dump it. Blocks of snow had to be loaded

Ton of Hay, by Parcel Post.

In the late winter of 1932, while the train was blocked by huge snow-slides, resourceful, stranded, Silverton residents decided to have 2 tons of hay that was needed to feed their livestock shipped in by U.S.Mail .
Living up to their slogan "The mail must go through," the Postal Service stamped and bundled the hay in Durango according to regulations, and carried the big load in by mule train.

The San Juan County Historical Society.

onto the same railroad cars that had brought the men to work, then hauled back up to Silverton and unloaded. In a move that garnered national publicity that spring, crews finally gave up on clearing away all the snow, and resorted to boring a tunnel through the snow slide for the train to pass through!

When Charles Bradshaw bought the line in 1981 he wanted to resume winter operations, though not all the way to Silverton. Winter service to Silverton, as history has shown, can be difficult, expensive, and dangerous. The D&SNG built

the Cascade Canyon Wye in 1981, and started winter service there that same year, avoiding the treacherous snow slides found farther to the north.

In the spring, MOW crews must remove slides from the tracks above Cascade Creek, sometimes an awesome and dangerous undertaking, despite their access to bulldozers and other modern equipment. The winter of 2004-05 saw record amounts of snow in the San Juans, much of it wet, heavy snow that created ideal conditions for avalanches. Slides that had been inactive for

The D&SNG utilizes heavy, modern equipment to clear rails. Michael (Moe) Rael carefully guides track hoe operator Pete Maisel onto a flat car near Silverton.

decades ran that winter, and the job awaiting D&SNG crews in the spring was daunting.

It is difficult to comprehend the huge scale of these slides until witnessing them personally. I was fortunate to visit the upper Animas gorge while tracks were being cleared. Many of the slides came down one side of the canyon, crossed the river, and went up the other! Even in mid-April, slides were still running and posing significant risk to workers.

Today, the D&SNG runs a winter train to Cascade Canyon Wye (check the schedule, as the frequency of operations changes during the winter season), so passengers have the opportunity to experience southwest Colorado's quiet, natural beauty at this time of the year.

During winter months you are likely to see herds of elk in the Animas Valley, and perhaps catch a glimpse of bald eagles perched in the cottonwoods along the river. Of course, you will also have the unique opportunity of witnessing a dramatic steam-powered locomotive in frosty weather—all from inside your warm, comfortable coach!

Using the railroad's D6 "Cat" bulldozer makes snow-clearing easier than it once was, but it is still a big job moving the wet, heavy snow. This photo was taken above Snowshed Slide, near MP 492.6, in the spring of 2005.

Monty Caudle clears off the turntable track during a heavy snow. Winter still provides logistical challenges for the D&SNG.

179

Railfest

Railfest is an annual celebration of special features for rail enthusiasts sponsored by the D&SNG since 1999, usually scheduled on the third weekend in August. Since its inception, Railfest has become a nationally recognized event attracting ever-increasing numbers of participants.

During Railfest, rides are offered on unique and historic equipment, like the Galloping Goose and the Eureka that would not be seen on rails anymore were it not for the support of this event by the D&SNG. Of course, the opportunity to ride this equipment on one of the most spectacular and scenic stretches of rail anywhere in the world is an added bonus. Railfest also offers special opportunities for photographers, along with displays and sales of railroad memorabilia.

Annually, in September and February, the D&SNG hosts a Photographer's Special.

The train and engine crews cater to serious shooters with photo run-bys at scenic spots all along the Durango-Silverton line.

The locomotive Eureka & Palisade #4, known simply as the Eureka, is a great attraction during Railfest. Locomotives like the Eureka that were designed in the early days of the West were colorful and brightly decorated. With its brass and copper fittings, polished walnut cab, and gold lettering, the Eureka may be the most photogenic narrow gauge locomotive in existence.

The Baldwin Locomotive Works built the beautiful wood-burning locomotive in 1875, and sent it to Nevada along the transcontinental railroad. It was used on the Eureka & Palisade line in central Nevada that operated between the two towns, Eureka and Palisade, from 1875 until 1901. It was then sold to a lumber company near Lake Tahoe that used the locomotive until 1939. The engine was then sent to San Francisco where it was to be sold for scrap, but was saved by a Warner Brothers studio employee for use as a movie prop. The Eureka was used in movies and television until 1976, and appeared in the last John Wayne movie, "The Shootist." It was featured in the Ken Burns documentary "The West."

Dan Markoff of Las Vegas, Nevada, purchased the locomotive after it was severely damaged—literally a hulk of iron and wheels— in a fire at a tourist resort in Nevada. The painstaking restoration project took six years.

The D&SNGRR Museum

Photographs by William Henry Jackson are mounted on the solid brick southern wall of the original roundhouse, most of which was destroyed by a fire in 1989.

The D&SNG museum is a tribute to railroading nationally, and especially in southwest Colorado.

The museum incorporates a wall of the original working roundhouse. It houses eight sets of tracks leading to the turntable outside and eight big sets of doors that formerly swung open for the big steam locomotives.

Two sets of track have been covered over to provide space for standing displays, while the remaining six are used for the exhibition of historic rolling stock, including the old RGS locomotive 42.

Historic and educational videos are shown in a passenger car that was used in the filming of "Butch

Cassidy and the Sundance Kid." Photography, both historical and contemporary, is presented throughout the museum.

The museum opened in 1998, and continues to add to its impressive, unique collection. A visit to the museum is a great way to enrich your understanding of the D&SNG and the fascinating history of railroading in southwest Colorado, as well as the cultural importance of the railroad throughout this country.

The D&SNG Museum is also a venue available for special events.

One Railroader's Story

John Hillier had direction early in his life: he was so impressed with the D&SNG on his first visit to Durango, when he was 5 years old, that he decided he wanted to work here, with the railroad. His dream has come to fruition; after moving to Durango from Florida when he was 21, John was hired as brakeman in 2004, and promoted to fireman for the 2005 season.

Working as a fireman is, of course, hard, physical work, but John enjoys the camaraderie he shares with the crews, and he says they try to have fun each day.

After his second season on the job, John offers some interesting firsthand observations on firing: "It's different every trip; different coal, different engineers, different trains. You always have to be right on top of it to do a good job, make as little smoke as possible, and not get ahead of yourself with too much steam or water. Firing downhill takes just as much planning ahead as firing uphill, it's just not as physically demanding. It takes almost a pound of coal per gallon of water, though that's not exact..."

John is representative of the many dedicated D&SNG employees who genuinely care about this railroad. As John says, "Everyone that works here is pretty different, but we do, mostly, have the railroad in common."

In May, 1987, John Hillier took his first ride on the D&SNG.

John "oiling around" during the summer of 2006.

183

I am very grateful for this opportunity to build on my first effort at telling the story of this unique and wonderful railroad.

Five years have transpired since printing the first edition of *America's Railroad*. The interim has been eventful and challenging for the D&SNG with big snows, big fires, new diesel locomotives, and much more. Through it all, the railroad has prevailed and prospered.

I salute all employees of the D&SNG! There is not space to mention all who deserve to be credited for their help on this project; nonetheless, a very special thanks goes out to Lynn Hutson, Dave Schranck, Jeff Ellingson, Kristi Nelson-Cohen, Rich Millard, and Steve Jackson.

I'll also take this opportunity to thank you, the passenger, for your continuing support of the D&SNG. You make all of this possible.

I hope to see you on the rails sometime soon!

Robert Royem

Sources:

Mining the Hardrock in the Silverton San Juans, John Marshall; Simpler Way Book Company, 1996.

Trails Among the Columbine, Steven J. Myers; Sundance Publications, Ltd., 1986.

A Historical Touring Guide of the San Juan Skyway, Ian Thompson; Ft. Lewis College, Office of Community Services, 1994.

A History of Southwestern La Plata County in Colorado, The Fort Lewis Mesa Reunion History Committee, 1991.

San Juan Country, Thomas M. Griffiths; Pruett Publishing, 1984.

Durango, Always a Railroad Town, Richard L. Dorman; R. D. Publications, Inc., 1996.

Rocky Mountain Boom Town, A History of Durango, Duane A. Smith; The University of New Mexico Press, 1980.

Silverton: A Quick History, Duane Smith; First Light Publishing, 1997.

Mountains of Silver: The Story of Colorado's Red Mountain Mining District, P. David Smith; Pruett Publishing, 1994.

Colorado 1870-2000 Revisited, Thomas J. Noel and John Fielder; Westcliffe Publishers, 2001.

Rebel of the Rockies; Robert G. Athearn; Yale University Press, 1962

The Rainbow Route: An Illustrated History, Robert E. Sloan and Carl A. Skowronski; Sundance Publications, Ltd, 1975.

Century of Struggle Against Snow: A History of Avalanche Hazard in San Juan County, Colorado, Betsy R. Armstrong; University of Colorado, 1976.

Narrow Gauge Railway Scenes, Adolf Hungry Wolf; Kromar Printing, Ltd., 1992.

Rio Grande Narrow Gauge, John B.
Norwood; Heimburger House
Publishing Company, 1983.

*Coal, Cinders, and Parlor Cars: A
Century of Colorado Passenger Trains,*
Editors: Charles Albi, R. C. Farewell,
William C. Jones; The Colorado
Railroad Historical Society, 1991.

*Robert W. Richardson's Narrow Gauge
News, Colorado Rail Annual No. 21,*
Editors: A. D. Mastrogiuseppe, Richard
A. Cooley, Charles Albi; The Colorado
Railroad Historical Society, 1994.

*A Ticket to Ride the Narrow Gauge,
Herbert Danneman; Colorado Rail
Annual No. 24,* Editors: Charles Albi,
Kenton Forrest, Robert Jensen; The
Colorado Railroad Historical Society,
2000.

*Many More Mountains, Volume 3: Rails
Into Silverton,* Allen Nossaman;
Sundance Publications, Ltd., 1998.
Rio Grande, Mainline of the Rockies,
Lucius Beebe and Charles Clegg;
Howell-North Books, 1962.

*Colorado Mining: A Photographic
History,* Duane Smith; University of
New Mexico Press; Albuquerque, NM,
1977.

*Many More Mountains, Volume 2: Ruts
into Silverton,* Allen Nossaman;
Sundance Publications, Ltd., 1993.

Out West; Mike Flanagan; Harry N.
Abrams, Inc, 1987.

This book was printed in Hong Kong by
Pacific Rim International.

**Museum Curator and renowned
watercolor artist, specializing in
railroads, Jeff Ellingson.**

Dave Schranck

2005 employee of the year Tony Garcia, left, with Jim Brittain.

Eric Nelson

Railfans, young and old.

Yvonne Lashmett

A tradition continues.

The D&SNG has inherited a rich and continuing, railroading legacy. From an auspicious beginning 125 years ago, the 45-mile Silverton Branch survived the lean times during the 1950s that witnessed the demise of most of America's railroads, largely through the devoted efforts of rail enthusiasts who were determined to preserve this spectacular remnant of mountain railroading. The D&SNG has also endured devastating natural and economic disasters through the years.

People have always made the difference with this railroad. Today the skilled, dedicated group of men and women working for the D&SNG is essential to its success. D&SNG employees all seem to enjoy their unique jobs and take pride in their accomplishments. They have a genuine affection for the railroad and its historical significance. From management on down, the D&SNG team takes seriously their responsibility of actively preserving, and improving this authentic cultural landmark.

The D&SNG works hard to be a good neighbor, listening to and addressing local concerns, and giving back generously to the local community. The railroad continues to enhance its service, adjusting to the changing priorities of society.

Along with the talented workforce, the hundreds of thousands of people from around the world who care about this railroad are also crucial to the D&SNG's continued health and prosperity. The railroad's operation would soon cease without the many passengers who are fortunate enough to visit southwest Colorado, and personally experience this vital link to America's past.

We call it America's Railroad, and it is a uniquely American creation, but the D&SNG is really a treasure for the world to enjoy and appreciate.